DREAM BIG

LIVE

BIGGER

DREAM BIG

LIVE

BIGGER

How to Change Your Life into a SUCCESS STORY

NOLAN R. BAUM

DEDICATION

To my beautiful and brilliant wife, Amber, who turned a good book into a great one.

To my mother

and

my grandparents for their guidance throughout my life.

"How does a young man capture and share such enduring wisdom? Nolan Baum is an "old soul" with a mission to disseminate transformational insights with all who will take the time to listen. Dream Big Live Bigger is an easily accessible compendium of timeless truths collected and stewarded by Nolan. It communicates inspiration and activates critical perspectives necessary to live a life of not just success but significance!"

-**JOSEPH MICHELLI**, New York Times #1 bestselling author of books like *The Starbucks Experience*, *Driven to Delight*, and *The New Gold Standard*

"I am not a fan of motivational, success/self-help books. But I have been very pleasantly surprised by the fast-paced writing style of this book, which offers sage advice in a very readable way. I look forward to going back through it."

-**RICK KRESS**, Kress Biblical Resources Publishing House

"Sometimes the best advice is often the simplest. Baum finds a way to culminate his life experiences into solid life advice for people of all ages who are looking for a better path. So often when reading books in this category you can feel like you're being talked down to. With this book...you feel like you are being talked with...I put it high on my recommend list."

-**NORM VAN NESS**, Chief Meteorologist, Broadcaster

CONTENTS

PREFACE

Everyone needs to read this book, regardless of your age or phase of life. It covers every topic from time management, money management, worrying, choosing a career, and much more.

Life is full of choices, and most of the time we don't know which way to go. This book won't give you the answers to all of life's questions, but it will lay out the framework for making those decisions. I honestly wish I had this book to guide me at a much earlier age.

This book does NOT consist of a lot of fluff. By that, I mean that it is not chock-full of theory and impractical lessons. This is an extremely practical, step-by-step guide to help you reach your fullest potential and live out your dreams.

Some points you may have heard before, but not in the way that this book delivers them. My lessons give real examples and rational reasoning that will stretch your thinking. This book will introduce you to new lessons that will help you live out your "dream big and live bigger" lifestyle. I want you to create your own success story.

INTRODUCTION

What is your biggest dream? You might have more than one, or even a list of them. Is it a smaller dream, a bigger one, a home with a white picket fence, or possibly visiting every country in the world? Maybe one of your dreams is to slow down and have more time to relax with your family. We all have dreams, but most of us are nowhere near to living them out. What is stopping us from living our dreams? This book will give you the tools you need to begin thinking and living bigger.

Could you imagine buying a one-way ticket to your favorite vacation spot, then staying as long as you want on vacation until you feel like going somewhere else? Most people go to Disney World and run around trying to see all the shows and ride all the rides trying to beat the clock because they only have that week to do so. Could you imagine going to Disney World for as long as you want? You could actually *relax* and enjoy your vacation. Most people have never thought about this scenario. Why not?

Why is the median household only making $49,000 a year? I bet if I asked them how much they would want to make they would tell me that they want to be millionaires instead. What is making them stay at $49,000 a year? Maybe they don't know how to live their dreams.

I've often wondered why people are the way they are. Why do they make the decisions that they do? Why aren't people living the dream life that they say they want to live?

This world is full of people who give up on their dreams every single day. There are few who make it past the starting line of the race, but most settle for just the warm up. If you stop after the warm up, you can't say that you ran the race, yet so many people claim they participated. If you aren't living your dreams, you know that merely saying you are content doesn't make it true. I'd say that people give up because they don't know the possibilities that are truly out there for them, nor do they realize their potential.

> "Compared to what we ought to be, we are only half awake. We are making use of only a small part of our physical and mental resources. Stating the thing broadly, the human individual thus lives far within his limits...He possesses powers of various sorts which he habitually fails to use."[1]
> –Professor William James of Harvard

Some people say that we only use 10% of our brains. I say that most only live 10% of their full potential in life. This book will give you the principles to unlock the other 90%.

It absolutely does not matter how high your IQ is; you can achieve more.

So ask yourself: What will happen if I don't live out my dreams?

Are you willing to let your dreams slip away? I'm here to tell you that you shouldn't because you don't have to. It's time to start living.

Fully Alive

Staring out the window of my apartment had become one of my favorite things to do in the morning. To the left was the Hollywood sign, straight forward was the Griffith Observatory, and to the right I would watch as the sun began to rise behind the skyscrapers of downtown Los Angeles. Because my apartment was in a tower, and I was one floor away from the very top of our building, I could see everything. There were city

Introduction

lights and palm trees as far as the eye could see. I was living a dream I never knew I had.

Rewind several years and I was sitting at the airport with my mother. Normally loved ones would have to say goodbye to you when you went through security, but my mom was a flight attendant. Not only was she allowed to see me to the gate, but we were able to skip all the long lines, and go straight through the non-revenue line.

She seemed pretty cool, calm, and collected considering that I was about to fly to Los Angeles with my last free flight. With no car, no job (not even an interview), and not knowing many people in California to rely on, I was making a pretty risky move. But yet, there we sat, unnaturally relaxed.

My mother had driven me to the airport many times full of tears and fear knowing that I would be gone for months on end. Why was this time different? I was about to move for an indefinite amount of time with a bag of clothes, toiletries, and seven hundred dollars in the bank. There was no telling when I would ever see her again; maybe in a year, maybe longer.

Instead of a sad and drawn out moment, she gave me a hundred dollar bill, hugged me, and said "good luck" as she watched me walk through the gate to my plane. I wasn't expecting any further financial support from my family.

Maybe she was accustomed to me traveling so much that she was desensitized; seeing me go was normal now? Perhaps that's why she was so calm. I was a young adult now, and maybe she wanted to show me that I wasn't her little boy anymore; she wanted to encourage me to be a man and learn to pick myself up by my own bootstraps.

Introduction

It wasn't until later in life that I found out why she was so calm. My mother said, "I assumed that you were going to fly home in just a couple of days." What I did was so radical and seemingly illogical that she thought it would never work, I would fail, and I would return to our small town in Ohio.

I had seen others get into a convertible and drive into the sunset as they were leaving everything behind, but that was only in the movies. I was moving for good. I had desires that were insatiable and too big for a small town.

In Ohio, opportunity wasn't exactly knocking on the door. I could get a job on the assembly line in a factory, or if I was lucky I could make a good living selling insurance; that's about it. I couldn't exactly use my gifts to their fullest potential.

I didn't grow up wealthy, and I never had many resources in and of myself to make my dreams come true right away. But I was looking for opportunities and within a few years, my story radically began to change.

Once I began to dream big and apply the principles in this book, I began to live bigger. I began to *create* experiences like never before. In a four year period I had been to sixteen different countries on five different continents. Never once did I travel with my family or a lot of money. I have:

• been chased by a herd of elephants
• jumped out of an airplane in Cape Town, South Africa
• zip-lined through the rain forest in Costa Rica
• gone through the Panama Canal
• been chased by hostile monkeys and was stranded at the train station in India
• taught a physical education class in Hong Kong
• toured the country playing the drums with an aggressive rock band

Introduction

I have countless stories, yet I never had a lot of money during these times. Needless to say, I came from humble beginnings.

Shortly after moving to Los Angeles, I was part of at least four start-up companies and within a few years, I found myself living in a high rise apartment in Hollywood driving sports cars. I am not saying that those were my goals in moving to California, but that's what happened.

I have lived an incredibly eventful life, and I have accomplished a lot of goals. This book will lay out the principles that helped me accomplish my goals and dreams, and it will give you the tools to help you attain yours.

A Life Worth Living

We are all familiar with the many rags to riches stories of those who lived in poverty before they became wealthy. You may be familiar with the example of John Paul Dejoria, co-founder of Paul Mitchell, who initially lived out of his car with seven hundred dollars to his name before becoming a billionaire.

A less known couple with a similar story as John Dejoria is one that I was fortunate enough to be mentored by in my early years.

In 1966, Charlie and Sandy were living in their first home. They had two children and no running water. As you can imagine, they had to make do with less.

They had an outhouse in their backyard and a coal furnace to stay warm during the harsh winters. There was no such thing as a thermostat, so Charlie had to put coals manually into their furnace to maintain the heat in the house.

Introduction

Charlie and Sandy did everything in their power to change their situation and to live out their dreams. Charlie worked at a factory during the week and sold items on the weekends. He sold soap door-to-door, and would also set up booths at local fairs to sell cleaning products. They didn't start with much; in fact, they utilized the very boxes that the cleaning products came in as chairs to sit on. You could say that Charlie tried it all when it came to sales, including selling cutlery and sweepers. Nothing sold well enough.

Now with a third child, Charlie and Sandy soon cut their losses and tried a brand new venture. With the skills and knowledge that they gained from their past experiences, Charlie and Sandy started their own business from scratch. Charlie still sold door-to-door, but this time was different.

With Charlie hitting the sidewalks and Sandy maintaining the office their income began to increase rapidly every year, and as you might guess, they got a new furnace.

Since they began living their dream, Charlie doesn't go to the store to buy bottled water; he hires a semi-truck to deliver the finest bottled water to his doorstep. He doesn't go to the mall to buy shoes; he has his shoes custom made to his feet and shipped to his home. He also has a tailor come to his office to fit him for suits.

Since age eleven, I sat at the feet of this couple who just so happened to be my grandparents. I wanted to learn about life, finances, and anything else that I could learn. It just so happened that they wanted to teach me.

Part 1:

Wisdom

1. LONG LIVE THE WISE

One of the best compliments one can ever receive is to be told that they are wise. Perhaps you have been told that you are an old soul; that's the same thing. To be thought of as older than you are, or to be told that you are more mature than your age, is a goal in itself.

As a young child, I always wanted to sit at the adult table. I rarely held enough in common with kids my age to hold a meaningful conversation. I also had a hard time fitting in with my age group as a young man. That was for many reasons; I didn't drink alcohol, I didn't play video games, nor did I watch television. That pretty much narrows the pool of possible friends for anyone, right?

I am not sure which side of the cause and effect law I was on. Maybe my older friends were an effect of my wisdom or maybe I was forced to hang out with older people because I didn't fit in with my peers. Regardless, I was, and still am, shaped by those around me, and so are you. Therefore, put yourself around older and more mature individuals to gain wisdom. Just know that older doesn't always mean more mature.

How does wisdom help you live your dreams? Wisdom is one of the four pillars:

Money
Time
Knowledge
Wisdom

...that creates possibilities. You must have all four to live your dream and sustain it. Some have won the lottery, so they have time and money, but they don't have the knowledge and wisdom necessary to keep the money.

Dream Big Live Bigger

Many people have enough time, money, and knowledge to do something or not to do something, but they are still unwise and act against what they know to be true, like buying the wrong house, dating the wrong person, etc.

Wisdom is the beneficial application of knowledge. Knowledge is knowing that you need to burn the same amount of calories as you consume. Wisdom is putting the fork down when or before your body tells you that you are full.

As the saying goes, "knowledge is knowing that a tomato is a fruit. Wisdom is not putting it in your fruit salad."

Humanly speaking, with money, time, knowledge, and wisdom almost anything is possible. That's a fact. There is pretty much nothing you can't do with these four elements. If I had enough time, money, knowledge, and wisdom I could interview the President of the United States of America, I could have the President interview me, or I could become the President. I don't think enough people would vote for me, but with wisdom perhaps I would easily know how to persuade others for their vote. Anyway, you get the point.

For the context of this book, focus every day on getting more time, money, knowledge, and wisdom. This book will teach you how. My list of the four pillars will now be mentioned in order of importance. Wisdom is absolutely the most important pillar.

Many have heard of arguably the richest man since the founding of the United States of America, John D. Rockefeller. Some estimate that Rockefeller's worth was 663.4 billion. There is one man who towers over his wealth, King Solomon. King Solomon's evaluated net worth was 2.1 trillion. Additionally, the Bible records that King Solomon was the richest and wisest man who ever lived.

Long Live the Wise

"...Behold, I give you a wise and discerning mind,
so that none like you has been before you and
none like you shall arise after you. I give you also
what you have not asked, both riches and honor,
so that no other king shall compare with you, all
your days."

–1 Kings 3:12-13

What is wisdom? There are many different definitions: Godly wisdom, worldly wisdom, and philosophical wisdom.

Which one is right?

According to the book *The Pilgrim's Progress*, worldly wisdom is chasing pleasure, ease, comfort, and safety. One could paraphrase this definition this way; worldly wisdom is only looking out for one's best interest. Everyone to some degree believes and lives by this definition, for better or for worse. I would argue for the worse. The problem lies in that most people don't know what truly is in their best interest. Somehow things get twisted; we usually end up doing things that harm us instead of help us. If we truly chased after our best interest, we could reach our full potential, but we get caught up in snares. I'll explain more about these snares later.[2]

One dictionary defines worldly wisdom as, "being prepared by experience for life's difficulties."[3] There is an issue with this definition as well. Usually, people don't learn from past experiences. Most don't learn from their past mistakes. Hoarders tend to keep hoarding, possessive spouses tend to stay possessive, and those in abusive relationships tend to cycle into a new abusive relationship. I call it insanity, but most people, by their actions, call it a way of life. As the well-known saying of George Wilhelm Friedrich Hegel goes, "there is one thing we learn from history, and that is that we learn nothing from history." Some do learn from their past or even better they learn from other peoples' mistakes. These are the exceptions, not the rule.

The second issue with the dictionary's definition is that we should never rely on our past experiences to help us with our life's difficulties. What if the lesson you learned was the wrong lesson? What if you never learned the right way to handle a similar situation in the future? We should never get our wisdom by how we responded in the past.

Philosophical wisdom started many schools of thought, which sprouted in ancient Greece by the droves. Someone would create a new belief, then convince their students and everyone else to follow them. It didn't matter how true their beliefs were.

Today we have the same kind of thing where people pay a lot of money to go to a famous school to get taught things that aren't necessarily true. You're probably safe with math, but when it comes to philosophy, politics, and religion we all need to be very discerning. A lot of these schools of thought are simply made up.

Philosophy is interesting to a small measure, but even Socrates said that he realized that he didn't know anything! "I am the wisest man alive, for I know one thing, and that is that I know nothing."
So let's not base our life decisions on philosophical wisdom. I suggest we need a more solid foundation.

Since King Solomon doubled the riches of the next wealthiest human being and he wrote parts of the Bible, namely most of Proverbs and all of Ecclesiastes, I have relied on his timeless wisdom to help me navigate through life.

Wisdom is needed to handle the other three pillars (time, knowledge, and money). Wisdom also saturates the whole book (ideally), but I will give a couple of characteristics of it now.

IT IS AVAILABLE, AND IT IS EVERYWHERE.

"Wisdom shouts in the street,
She lifts her voice in the
square;
At the head of the noisy
streets she cries out."

–Proverbs 1:20

Wisdom is the *most* important pillar.

Part 2:

TIME

2. LIVE LIKE YOU'RE DYING

The next pillar we need to address is time. In order to think bigger we need to appreciate time for what it is and understand its effects.

Is Time On Your Side?

To live your dreams and reach your full potential you need to make the most out of your extremely short life. Is it possible to have time on your side? Financially, maybe, but time is one of your worst enemies. Time is never really on your side. Time is not your friend, it is not your buddy, and it is never for you.

Time is moving fast. You have to move faster.

We're constantly racing against the clock. I ran track in high school. Sometimes I was the underdog in a race, but sometimes I was likely to win. When I was anticipated to win, my coach always told me that I was racing against the clock instead of against the other school. He was right. Even when there isn't direct human competition, time is always against you.

Time is the competitor that never loses. You cannot win against time. In life there are no 're-dos' or 'start-over buttons.' Time just keeps taking and taking and taking.

Time is valuable. The reason it is valuable is because it is valued by all and is only lost, not added. In that sense, time is the scarcest commodity in existence.

We need to be extreme because time is extreme. Time doesn't wait for anything. It is unforgiving. I couldn't be any more serious; time is literally killing you. Let me explain, the cells in your body are dying. Apoptosis is unexplainable, programmed cell death. In this case, the cell commits suicide simply because time told it to, and this process is irreversible. The process of apoptosis produces the effects of senescence, or biological aging, a.k.a. getting old.

We want to be able to look back at our lives and smile, not withdraw in shame, tears, or even disgust because of how we wasted our time.

If you want to know how valuable time is, just ask a soldier who was deployed while his little child took his first step. Ask a dad who has to reschedule a wedding anniversary celebration or he might lose his job. Time is one of the most precious and delicate resources we have. It is non-refundable once it is spent; you cannot buy more. You were born at an appointed time, and you will die at an appointed time.

Consider time as more valuable than money. You can earn money, but you can't earn more time. You can lose money and get it back. Every second that passes is gone forever.

YOU ONLY LIVE ONCE

I fully understand that you can argue with this section heading, *You Only Live Once*, but you do only live on this earth once. Since this is a reality that we all have to face, it seems fully logical that in this lifetime you would want to strive for excellence. There are no re-dos, so this life is yours to manage. How good of a manager will you be?

THE BELL CURVE

We really need to be conscious of getting old because our value to society is directly coordinated to our age. Picture a bell curve. When you are a young child, you don't bring much value to society. Therefore, you don't get compensated very much. As you get older, you begin to have the capabilities, and the physical and mental capacities to add value and make money. Then of course, as you get older the slope of the curve gets steeper. Before you know it, it is time for you to retire because you are no longer useful to society.

We can't control when we are born, and we pretty much can't control when we die, this is the rule—there are exceptions of course. So, the point is to get to our peak on the bell curve as fast as we can and stay there as long as we can. To do that you will need to keep reading.

The Great Equalizer

Time is the one thing everyone has in common. Everyone on the planet Earth, who ever lived, has had the same amount of time in a day. Therefore, everyone needs to pay close attention to this part of the book.

Life is not fair in any respect. Everyone is made differently; for example, body types are something that we can't change. You are a mesomorph, endomorph, or ectomorph. Fundamentally this is what body type you are, and no matter what you do, you can only change your body so much.

If your foot is most compatible with a size eighteen shoe, you have to buy a size eighteen shoe if you want it to fit properly. There's no natural way around it, which unfortunately for most people seems unfair, especially for the individual with that large of feet.

No two people are exactly the same. We don't have the same amount of good looks, intellect, mechanical ingenuity, and so on.

Time is the great equalizer.

3. AVOID WASTING TIME

"Resolved, that I will live so, as I shall wish I had done when I come to die." –Jonathon Edwards

If you're doing what you ought to do, you won't have time to do the things you ought not to do....don't waste time.

LIFE WILL WASTE YOUR TIME

Things in life are wasting your time already, like being stuck in traffic for two hours, being sick in bed, or waiting for your doctor at the doctor's office. There are enough things wasting your time; don't add to the waste.

SLEEPING

How many hours do billionaires sleep? Donald Trump has repeatedly said that he only sleeps about four to five hours a night. Maybe you are like me, and you need around nine hours. I wish that I could live and function off of less sleep because if time is money, then sleep is very expensive. I wish I didn't need to sleep at all.

Is there a way to train your body to get less sleep and still function at the same efficiency? The military probably believes so, but my research shows that you can't stay at the same efficiency. (Disclaimer: I'm not a doctor)

Napoleon is alleged to have said that sleeping is for the weak, but in fact, he, himself, got plenty of sleep. Research shows that,
> "...there are a few very rare individuals who can manage with only five hours of sleep a night without experiencing deleterious effects. They are sometimes known as the "sleepless elite." In 2009, a team led by geneticist Ying-Hui Fu at the

University of California San Francisco discovered a mother and daughter who went to bed very late, yet were up bright and early every morning. Even when they had the chance to have a lie-in at the weekend (a tell-tale sign that you are sleep-deprived) they didn't take it. Tests revealed that both mother and daughter carried a mutation of a gene called hDEC2. When the researchers tweaked the same gene in mice and in flies, they found that they also began to sleep less –and when mice were deprived of sleep they didn't seem to need as much sleep in order to catch up again. This demonstrates that genetics play at least some part in your need for sleep."[4]

We might not all have this special hDEC2 gene, so for now we'll have to continue getting our eight to nine hours. But don't worry; there are a lot of areas in our lives that we can cut back on to save time.

WHAT ARE YOU READING?

Read as much as you can, but don't waste your time with fictional or fantasy books if you don't have to. Reading fictitious books is essentially the same as watching television shows. Although reading is a little better because your brain needs to process words, and translate them into thoughts; which increases your reading comprehension for reading in the future. But reading fictitious books still puts you in a trance. It doesn't directly help you move the financial and emotional snowball down the hill. Instead, read books that will teach you something that you will use within the next six months or less—like this book.

Arguing Opinions and Debating

Never argue opinions. Everyone thinks they have a *need* to be right. We can debate the reasons behind this, but then we would be proving my point. Learn to back down from an argument, because the truth is, there is no right, or wrong; they are just opinions.

No one wins an argument. If you lose the argument, then you lose. If you win the argument, then you still lose. Let me explain. The winner of the argument still loses because he loses the fellowship with the one holding the opposing viewpoint. The friend who lost the argument will usually have resentment. It is rare to win an argument and keep a friend.

Never tell people that they are wrong, but always admit when *you* are wrong. This immediately defuses any situation. It is hard for people to be mad at you when you are "mad" at yourself. It doesn't sound like that makes sense, but that's reality. Human beings rarely do things that make logical sense.

Let people finish their thoughts –all of them. Even when you think they are done saying their thoughts, wait a few seconds because they probably have thoughts in their head still. If you don't, they won't listen to you because they are distracted by the thoughts that are still in their heads.

Because people need to be right, make sure you focus on what you *agree* with them on as much as possible; so that everyone can win and no one wastes time.

Arguing opinions are one of the biggest wastes of time that I can think of. Whenever I hear the words, "I think," followed by a point that I disagree with, I will say something like, "That's definitely one way of looking at it," or, "You got a point there."

Dream Big Live Bigger

Even though I completely disagree with them I will acknowledge that they have the right to have an opinion. Whatever you do, do not waste your time arguing because you have a different opinion. Frankly, who cares?

Instead of responding with a contrary opinion, ask a question like, *"have you heard the other opinions on it?"* Be as agreeable as possible, but make sure that you're not lying. Do your best to agree and affirm the other person even if it's just, "yeah I heard that, have you heard the other side of it?" This will save a lot of frustration and, more importantly, a whole lot of time.

To reiterate my points in other words, I'll share a source that I found to be useful. In an article in Bits and Pieces, *some suggestions are made on how to keep a disagreement from becoming an argument:

Welcome the disagreement. Remember the slogan, "When two partners always agree, one of them is not necessary." If there is some point you haven't thought about, be thankful if it is brought to your attention. Perhaps this disagreement is your opportunity to be corrected before you make a serious mistake.

Distrust your first instinctive impression. Our first natural reaction in a disagreement situation is to be defensive. Be careful. Keep calm and watch out for your first reaction. It may be you at your worst, not at your best.

Control your temper. Remember, you can measure the size of a person by what makes him or her angry.

Listen first. Give your opponents a chance to talk. Let them finish. Do not resist, defend or debate. This only raises barriers. Try to build bridges of understanding. Don't build higher barriers of misunderstanding.

Avoid Wasting Time

Look for areas of agreement. When you have heard your opponents out, dwell first on the points and areas on which you agree.

Be honest. Look for areas where you can admit error and say so. Apologize for your mistakes. It will help disarm your opponents and reduce defensiveness.

Promise to think over your opponents' ideas and study them carefully. And mean it. Your opponents may be right. It is a lot easier at this stage to agree to think about their points than to move rapidly ahead and find yourself in a position where your opponents can say: "We tried to tell you, but you wouldn't listen."

Thank your opponents sincerely for their interest. Anyone who takes the time to disagree with you is interested in the same things you are. Think of them as people who really want to help you, and you may turn your opponents into friends.

Postpone action to give both sides time to think through the problem. Suggest that a new meeting be held later that day or the next day, when all the facts may be brought to bear. In preparation for this meeting, ask yourself some hard questions:

Could my opponents be right? Partly right? Is there truth or merit in their position or argument? Is my reaction one that will relieve the problem, or will it just relieve frustration? Will my reaction drive my opponents further away or draw them closer to me? Will my reaction elevate the estimation good people have of me? Will I win or lose? What price will I have to pay if I win? If I am quiet about it, will the disagreement blow over? Is this difficult situation an opportunity for me?

*Bits and Pieces, published by The Economics Press, Fairfield, N.J.[5]

Philosophy

We have all heard of Socrates, Plato, and Aristotle, and we sound very sophisticated when we quote them. The problem with philosophy is that it is essentially the study of someone's opinion on any given subject matter. Philosophy then is the art—to a large degree—of making up definitions to made-up phrases.

For example, philosophers have been arguing their opinions on free will, morality, and love for thousands of years. This cycle is never going to end because they are just opinions that have turned into beliefs over time.

Maybe reading Thomas Reid stimulates your brain and makes you contemplate your navel, but I would submit to you that there are more important and profitable subjects to study. I am not saying not to have a basic knowledge of philosophy, but I am saying not to base your beliefs on their opinions.

I was flying to Los Angeles sitting next to an older man. Seeing that he was reading a religious book, I naturally started a conversation with him. It turns out that he was a Professor of Religion and Politics at a top university.

He began to tell me about how his students loved his class on interpreting the Bible through the lens of a Greek philosopher.

Greek philosophy basically says that the physical is bad, and the spiritual is good. They also taught that the obvious meaning of a text is not the true meaning and that you need to find the deeper meaning. There, now you know everything you need to know about Greek philosophy. I digress.

Avoid Wasting Time

A big smile went on his face, and he proceeded to tell me how I needed to reinterpret what all of the numbers in the Bible meant. For example, the number 10 isn't really a literal amount; it's an analogy for something else. Shaking my head, I told him that you can't interpret the Bible however you please, even though some philosophers want to.

Just understand that in philosophy there are no absolute truths, and let me repeat, debating opinions is pretty much a waste of time.

Thomas Reid was part of the "Scottish common sense school of philosophers" that lived in the seventeen hundreds. Many would argue that he was known for "his defense of Agent Causation in the free will debate."[6]

Anyway, Thomas Reid wrote an essay called *The Liberty of Moral Agents*. In it he states,

> "If, in any action, he had power to will what he did,
> or not to will it, in that action he is free. But if in
> every voluntary action, the determination of his
> will be the necessary consequence of something
> involuntary in the state of his mind, or of
> something in his external circumstances, he is not
> free."[7]

So let's get this straight, you only have free will if there are no internal or external forces that are influencing you to make that choice? So essentially there is no free will in his argument. I would also add that the phrase free will is a made up concept, but that's for another book –research it if you don't believe me.

My point is, why do I care about someone's opinion of free will? Because it makes you think? There are a lot of made-up definitions to a lot of made-up phrases.

You can easily get distracted, and before you know it you have just wasted precious time that you could have used productively. You're probably not going to change anyone's opinion. If I had convinced that religion and politics professor that he was teaching strange lessons, he would have to change his entire class. Maybe I made him think, but I think I just annoyed him. After our conversation, he indicated clearly that he didn't want to talk to me anymore.

Commercials

Time is a precious commodity. When you spend time, it better yield a profit. Don't give it away for free.

Avoid watching and listening to commercials at all costs. Commercials waste time. Corporations need to pay me for my time to listen to their sales pitch. My time is way too valuable to watch commercials, and so is yours.

The job of advertisers is to make you dissatisfied and discontent with what you have so that you will buy their products.

Advertisers are very good at brainwashing, and making free advertisers out of you. Commercials take many forms, such as the song at the beginning of a television show. Many people can recite the song that they play before their favorite show. Perhaps you can recite multiple, which provides evidence to my point. I bet you are singing one of the jingles right now. This needs to end. Turn off all commercials, and literally never listen to them. Frantically find the remote and change the channel or turn the television off. Do you think I'm being extreme? Advertising is extreme. Do you have any idea how much money goes into the business?

Advertisers are professional manipulators; they do it well and often, and I really don't want them to influence my habits or thoughts. I also don't want to have a jingle stuck in my head, and catch myself singing it out loud; thereby becoming an advertiser for them and not getting paid for it.

Commercials take time away. You could be thinking, planning, debriefing, or scheduling during those thirty seconds to a minute. You might even get an idea for a new invention, but at the very least you're not giving your precious time away for free.

This principle also applies to computer ads. Get an ad-blocker app for your computer. Trust me. You will be less distracted, you will be more productive, and you will be way more successful in life.

Don't Worship False Idols

Worshiping idols is both consuming and enslaving. Idols will hold you back from reaching your full potential. It's a good idea for me to go ahead and give a basic understanding of what worship is. One of the best and most practical ways to define worship is that it is what you spend a lot of your: time, perhaps money, and focus on; and you refuse to give it up. Whatever came to mind as you read that is probably your idol.

There is a huge field of idols to choose from. In this day and age, there seem to be a growing number of distractions that we can choose to worship, things we can't go without: television shows, sports, bad relationships, etc. You need to identify them and get rid of them. You might need some help. If you can't cut your cable, or do whatever it takes to stop the enslavement, you will be your own worst nightmare, and you will be the reason you don't reach your full potential.

Never waste your time worshipping an individual, such as an actor or professional athlete. Don't be distracted with worshipping, or looking up to these stars to the point of idolizing them. It's one thing to find enjoyment alongside others at a baseball game, and another to obsess. Pour into the people around you, not into non-existing relationships. Your idol doesn't even know that you exist in order to care about you.

If you catch yourself paying a lot of money, and spending a lot of time going to an event to see a group of people perform, be careful. Going to a sports event is obviously not some grave sin, but if you find yourself raising your hands and making loud emotional praises—you may be crossing over into worship. Just sayin'.

Are you able to miss a game? Do you spend your hard-earned money buying objects with "your" team's name on it? Ask yourself if you get mad if "your" team loses. Consider which "relationships" are worth spending your time on and how much of it.

NARCISSISM

You can make yourself into your own idol. According to myth, Narcissus' beauty was unmatched by any other. He was loved and sought after by many, though he found none worthy of his love or desire. At one point in the myth, Narcissus falls upon the gaze of his reflection in a lake. He is so utterly captivated by his own beauty that he can't leave his reflection. At the end of the tale, Narcissus dies at the lake, never able to leave his love for himself.

Avoid Wasting Time

Being narcissistic is what I call a mind distraction. Mind distractions waste your time and energy.

Mind distraction is a term that I have coined to mean a distraction that only happens in your thoughts with no external source provoking it at all. There are a lot of things that want to distract you, and we've already addressed a few, but like it or not we want to distract ourselves. We can be in a silent study room with no noise or pictures and still be completely distracted. Instead of working, you are thinking about unrelated things. Those are what I call mind distractions.

One of these mind distraction is thinking about how great you are, narcissism.

Don't be distracted by *you*.

Avoid being narcissistic by listening more than speaking. Only share your accomplishments when you have a pertinent point.

Don't be consumed by your looks, or having pictures of yourself everywhere. Most of us are not professionally paid models so we should probably limit our selfies. Again, this is the rule; there are exceptions, e.g. for the sole purpose of marketing.

Don't boast of your past accomplishments *or* boast in your sufferings. Some people love to remind others how much they have been through, and how they are such a strong person. But the very fact that they have to convince others of this reveals that they are actually not a strong person because they need validation from others. Narcissism takes its form in thinking too much about yourself and trying to have everyone else thinking about you as well.

Avoid Unnecessary Competition

When we think about competition what are some examples that we normally think of? Typically, we think of playing a sport like basketball or hockey. The game ends and life goes on. It is great exercise and you learn great social skills, like how to share and encourage the other teammates. This kind of competition is beneficial, but there are other types of competition that are pointless and a huge waste of time.

Don't get distracted by pointless, petty competition. Stay on track to reach your goals. There are countless examples of unnecessary competitions, like speeding ahead of someone to change lanes. Even arguing your point is usually an unnecessary competition. Any competition that has no actual benefit, and has no real consequences if you lose, is an unnecessary competition.

As you may have noticed, I am specifying that unnecessary competition is, well, unnecessary. However, there are necessary competitions. We will have to compete in our work fields. We will have to compete against others for the one open position. There is nothing wrong with healthy, natural competition. I am not advocating that you passively or submissively refrain from competition at all costs, and I am not asking you to ignore all other relevant information regarding the application of wisdom.

Healthy competition will help you grow and will show you the areas that you may be weak in or gifted in. If the average person can't perform as well as you in a given task, it may convey that you are above average in your skill level. Take this and hone in on it; this is where you have been gifted.

Avoid Wasting Time

I have heard it said by many motivational speakers that you are only competing with yourself. In fact, I heard it this past week at an audition for a convention. The fact is, you are *never* competing against yourself, regardless of what others say. You compete with others and time; there are always other competitors. You might have wars rage inside of yourself. You might be battling sin, but I would call that a war, not a competition.

As nice as it would be to be competing against yourself only, it doesn't hold true, especially in the workforce. Yes, you should challenge yourself. Yes, you should push yourself and yes, you should accept that you may not be as gifted as the next guy. Unfortunately, you are competing with others in some form, because not everyone will be hired, chosen, or wealthy.

Making the distinction between necessary, beneficial competition and unnecessary, time-wasting competition is absolutely crucial. We will always want to look at other people as a competitor; even when they don't need to be. It is innate in our nature. Becoming embittered when our competition rises above us is where the larger problem cultivates. The more competitive you get, the more distracted you get, thus the more time you waste.

Comparing Yourself to Others

Sometimes it's a good idea to compare ourselves to others; sometimes it's not.

It is good to compare yourself to others if you are heading down a bad path, or if you can't seem to get ahead in life. One example is comparing yourself to others to evaluate your spending habits. If the lower class is spending money on X, Y, and Z, maybe you shouldn't; unless you want to be lower class. If you are spending your time and money on things that mainly only poor people buy, you will have a difficult time getting ahead. Once you get to an event or store, look around you. Chances are, if only teenagers are there, you should not be—even if you are a teenager. You want to spend your time and money wisely.

Another example of comparing yourself to others for the right reason is to see if your friends are holding you back. Examine your friends. If birds of a feather flock together, then look around you. What are their habits? How do they spend their time? If they waste a lot of time, and you're hanging out with them, guess what, you're probably wasting just as much time. It might be *time* for new friends.

DON'T COMPARE YOURSELF WITH OTHER PEOPLE UNNECESSARILY

If you are going to compare yourself to others, don't compare yourself to people your age. Find someone older and wiser to compare yourself to, so that you can learn from them and aim high. For this, the point is to become like the one you compare yourself to, which is a profitable thing. If you desire to provide well for your family (or future family), compare yourself to the facts.

Let's do a real comparison. According to the IRS, in 2010-2014, the top 1% of Americans made $380,354 annually. The top 5% only made $159,619. You'll realize that once you begin to see how much they actually make, it's not that hard to get into the top 1%. It's not an elusive, unattainable amount of money. Only compare yourself to others in such a way that it is productive and encouraging.[8]

Criticize Not, Lest Ye Be Criticized

"Criticizing doesn't bring about lasting changes and often incurs resentment."[9]–Dale Carnegie

My mother always told me, "If you don't have anything nice to say, don't say anything at all." It is true. It works.
Naturally, everyone thinks that they are a good person. People aren't going to condemn themselves. Therefore, criticizing is pointless, and often puts people on the defense. It doesn't help and it's not productive.

Don't consume your thoughts with belittling or criticizing others. Don't look for their flaws. This is especially difficult for analytical people and insecure people who criticize others to puff up their own pride.

Criticizing others is a mind distraction, is entirely unproductive, and wastes a lot of time. Perhaps you think that you only waste a few seconds or minutes a day doing this, but think of how much we gossip. Pretty much every time we talk about someone behind their backs we are criticizing them. What do you talk about when you get around your friends or family? We all gossip to some measure, the goal is to taper that down. The truth is that this is another example of comparing yourself to others unnecessarily.

Here is another example; we all naturally skim a room to analyze others who we instinctively believe are our competitors in some way. We are looking for flaws, strengths, and basically anything in anyone that could threaten our possessions or our pride.

Dream Big Live Bigger

The goal, subconsciously or consciously, is to figure out how much better we are than them, but the problem is that believing that you are better isn't good enough. We feel this need to criticize them so that others know how much better we are. If there is someone who might be "better" than you, we have a problem and we feel insecure. There is no benefit to scanning the room; it is only a mind distraction. This is particularly obvious the first day of school or work when we choose where to sit at for lunch, or when you walk into a restaurant in a small town. The amount we skim the room is a litmus test of how secure and confident we are. Trust me on this one.

I understand that controlling your thoughts takes a lot of discipline, but if you are focused on what you should be focused on, it becomes easier. Reading this book (multiple times if necessary) will help with that.
Here is the tough part. People are very sensitive. It does not matter if you intend to criticize someone or not, if someone feels offended by your comments they will use that "loving correction" against you. If you criticize others, intentionally or not, they will use it against you. (I will touch on correcting others later).

If you tell someone that it's better not to watch television, they will be watching you to make sure that you're not watching television, even if not watching T.V. wasn't the point you were originally trying to make. Everyone does this, but the less you criticize others, the more successful you will be, and the less time you will waste.

Peer Pressure

Don't give into peer pressure. *Never* do things just because others want you to. If you are going to Sunday morning 'Mass' to practice Catholicism, make sure you know about Catholicism. Have a solid reason for the things you do. Don't do things just because others are pressuring you into doing it.

There are a lot of examples of this occurring within fraternities, clubs, various organizations, or affiliations. Join, attend, and serve because you want to, not because all of your peers pressure you. Be intentional with all of your thoughts and actions. Whatever you do, know why you're doing it, and make sure it is strategic. Don't waste your time doing things you wouldn't normally do because your friends or family want you to. This principle will save you hours a week.

Placing Blame

Don't waste time placing blame. Some have an urge and passion for pinning their frustration on someone. Most people do. They feel like they are accomplishing something when in actuality they are misplacing valuable energy. Instead, these people should be finding solutions.

Some managers or employers feel like they must find out every single detail of what happened before they fix the problem. They need to know who did it, why they did it, and force them to admit that they did it. Sometimes this could be necessary, but it's mostly a huge waste of time. Typically this interrogation is not necessary because the person who made the mistake already knows what he or she did wrong and the solution to it. They don't need to waste a day or two being told how to fix it. Fixating on placing blame doesn't help anyone.

We can't change other people; we've all tried one time or another, but what we can do is work on ourselves. You may not be able to force your manager to chill out, but you can end the distraction and time wasting by not placing the blame on other people. Find a way to take some ownership if you had any part in it. If you weren't involved, give people the benefit of the doubt and move on.

4. HOW TO STOP WORRYING

"My life has been full of terrible misfortunes. Most of which never happened."[10] –French philosopher, Montaigne

I was on a flight to Los Angeles and I happened to sit next to Quinton Flynn. Quinton is a professional voice actor and a super nice guy. The entire five and a half hour flight consisted of him doing impressions of different actors and ordering us drinks in the voice of Christopher Walken and Christopher Lloyd.

One of the characters that Quinton did the voice acting for was Timon from Timon and Pumbaa. If you have ever seen The Lion King you'll know the song they sing, Hakuna Matata. "Hakuna Matata, what a wonderful phrase. It means no worries for the rest of your days." We might not all have a "problems free philosophy", but we definitely need to have "no worries."

Worrying is always unnecessary, and it always wastes precious time and energy. Be concerned and take logical action to protect yourself and others, but don't be anxious. To reach your fullest potential and live bigger, you need to learn how to fight your worry battle the right way.

Worrying is *No* Rocking Chair

There is a very popular quote that states, "Worrying is like a rocking chair. It gives you something to do, but it doesn't get you anywhere." Let me be the first to tell you that worrying is not like a rocking chair, it's more like bleeding yourself to death. It is deadly. People have no idea how worrying ruins their lives and the lives of those around them. One dictionary defines worry as, "to torment oneself with or suffer from disturbing thoughts."[11] That's a pretty good definition.

The Effects of Worry on Your Body

How does worrying affect your brain? How does it affect your emotions?

Can worrying kill you? Is it possible to worry yourself to death?

Worry has the potential to do more than just poison your thoughts; it also can create a toxic environment for your entire body. When you worry, you put your body in a state of fight or flight. This looks like a shift in gears from the autonomic nervous system being at rest to being fully heightened.

Problems arise when the body stays in this state and doesn't shift back. Worry keeps your body from rest. It allows your system to stay heightened until it wears itself out.

WORRYING IS NOT A HABIT

Most people have a false understanding of what worry is. They are influenced by psychologists, or what the most popular book tells them.

One book on worrying defines it as a habit that needs to be broken—that was the only definition that I found in the entire book. This same book that poorly defines 'worry', sells millions of copies. It is clear that people worry and they want to know how to stop it, but they are found wanting. If that is you, please keep reading.

What is a habit? Could worry be a habit? We liked our last definition from the online dictionary site, so let's grab another. This dictionary defines a habit as "an acquired behavior pattern regularly followed until it has become almost involuntary."[12] So if worrying is indeed a habit, then it is probably involuntary and it's not an intentional act of the will. If worry is a habit, then those who fall prey to its irresistible power are trapped, with no chance of escape. If that's true, there is no hope. I know that people can break habits, but my point is that worrying is not an involuntary act, it is very voluntary and there is hope.

FORGETTING IS *NOT* THE ANSWER

Countless books and poems that I have read on this topic suggest that we should forget about the past and stop thinking about tomorrow; though they say this in different ways. In other words, just shut yesterday's and tomorrow's worries off. Well, you can't simply forget about the past, and telling people not to worry about the past or the future isn't really a solution. What they are saying is, 'just stop worrying.' Sorry, but that is lacking in reason and logic. If you see phrases like, 'you just need to live for today,' know that that person just wasted a couple seconds of your day as you read and perhaps validated (hopefully not) this same falsehood.

DISTRACTION IS *NOT* THE ANSWER

Some believe that if they focus hard enough on a particular task, they will stop worrying. There are a lot of stories of how people overcame worry by distracting themselves with work, school, vacations, and so on. This is not the true solution, but more like putting a Band-Aid on a gunshot wound.

Distracting yourself is like the ostrich putting his head in the sand. You are only pretending that the worry is not there, you're not actually dealing with it.

RESOLVING NOT TO WORRY IS *NOT* THE ANSWER

Some people do come to the rational resolution that worrying is illogical because it doesn't help you at all. Unfortunately, that is not a solution to stop worrying, although it should be the motivation to learn how to stop. Resolving not to worry is synonymous with telling yourself not to worry, and telling yourself not to worry is not a solution.

TELLING YOURSELF, "THINGS COULD BE WORSE" IS *NOT* THE ANSWER

Telling yourself that things could be worse is not the solution, but it may help humble you. Humility is definitely a step in the right direction.

A FATALIST ATTITUDE IS *NOT* THE ANSWER

Fatalism is the passive acceptance of the inevitable. We don't want to be passive about anything. People will tell you, "just accept it." We need to actively eradicate worry, not passively accept that we are victims of inevitable doom.

STOPPING WHEN YOU HIT A CERTAIN POINT IS *NOT* THE ANSWER

Some believe that you need to choose a point in which you will just stop worrying. When this boils down, you are just telling yourself not to worry, and telling yourself *not* to worry is not a solution.

SAYING "IT MIGHT NOT HAPPEN" IS *NOT* THE ANSWER

Thinking of the probability of something happening might distract you from your worry, but it does not cure you. Distractions only work for a limited amount of time and are not going to weed out the underlying problem. You are merely feeding your mind statistics to cloud out your worrying. A plane is highly unlikely to crash, which automatically means that the individual worrying has an irrational fear. Believe it or not, irrational fears cannot be fought with statistics. Statistics are for rational fears.

Now, don't get me wrong, I'm *not* saying that we shouldn't use probabilities in our calculated decisions, it *is* the best information we have to make our decisions. What I am saying is not to misuse statistics to feed your desires for control in order to alleviate irrational worry. Did you catch that? *The real problem with worry is the desire for control.*

The Truth Behind Why We Worry

There are many popular concepts of what worry is and why we have it.

There is no *magical* formula for solving the worrying problem, but there is a very simple one.

If you want something, don't have total control of the situation, and there is a probability of you not getting what you want, you will worry. Putting it into an equation:

Worry = want + lack of control + probability of not getting what you want

WANT

It's ok to want something, and you should want certain things. You should want to eat, take care of your family, work hard, etc. And, as I will explain in more detail later in this book, we always want something, and we always and only do what we want to do.

Even Buddhists know that wanting is part of the equation that leads us to worry and discontentment. One of the four noble truths is to get rid of all desire. They strive their entire lives to get rid of all desires. Well, that is not logical. How can you desire to get rid of desires?

OUT-OF-CONTROL

We all want to be in control. We never want to be told what to do, and we want to be the masters of our own little world. The truth is that you don't have complete control over anything.

Did you have control over:

Where you were born?

When you were born?

How to Stop Worrying

How you were born?

What ethnicity you were born into?

Which nation you were born in?

How tall you are?

Who your parents are?

Who your brothers and sisters are?

What kind of personality or temperament you have?

Who your grandparents are?

What food you like?

What activities you enjoy?

Do you have ultimate control now over:

Your car from breaking down?

If you get cancer?

When you will die?

I don't believe in chance or luck and neither should you. Nothing happens by accident. God is sovereign; he is in complete control, and guess what, he has never worried about anything, ever.

NOT GETTING WHAT YOU WANT

When it comes to not getting what we want, grown-ups are just like little children. We whine, we get mad, and we seek revenge. I for one, get pouty and irritable when I don't get enough sleep. We tend to respond emotionally when we do not get what we want.

How to Actually Stop Worrying

"Of course, the sovereign cure for worry is religious faith."
–William James, former professor of philosophy at Harvard[13]

When you are still in the struggle of want becoming a demand, while fully aware that you may not get it, let go of the demand. Offer your desires up to God. Let go of them because they are not yours to hold so tightly onto. Accept it. It's okay to have the desire, but you must have it with an open palm. Feed yourself the truth. Munch on the realities of the character of the One who is in control. Then entrust yourself, complete with every desire, to Him. If you don't, you take on an unnecessary burden of worrying. This is always the result that comes from demanding what you have no control over. I'm not going to convince you of this, but you would benefit from accepting it.

HUMBLE ACCEPTANCE

Accept the fact that you're not in control. Let that sink deep into your mind. The reason is that the equation will never change, and you will never be in control. You will always be out of control, and even more than you realize.

TRUST

Trust in the one who is in control. This is done by understanding God's sovereignty and goodness. What is trust? I trust him because I know that he knows everything, has the power to actuate his will, and he has my best interest in mind. Trusting God rather than fighting him for control (that I don't and won't have) is always liberating.

SELFISHNESS

Ultimately the reason we worry about our future is that we are self-centered, self-absorbed, and selfish. I'm preaching to myself especially. I'm the master at worrying.

I've had to make tough decisions in my life, and that's when worry typically kicks in. When I get stuck in that trap, I think logically. I ask myself what my options are and what I can do about the issue. I try to collect as much information as possible, but I know that I won't have all the information. I also know that all I can do is make a calculated decision. Before, during, and after I get trapped in my worry I read the Bible, remind myself of God's promises, and pray.

Worrying is focusing all of your attention on yourself. Take time to think of others; this is easier said than done. Look for opportunities to serve. Help someone move, or call a friend to see how they are doing, etc. Helping others can be used as a distraction, so be careful. Don't serve others in order to stop worrying. Rather, remind yourself that being self-absorbed promotes all things that lead to worry. Help others, do your part in the matter, give up ultimate control, and trust God for the results.

5. HOW TO USE YOUR TIME WISELY

Distraction Abatement

Now that we've addressed what not to do, let's talk about what we need to be doing to live to our full potential.

Next, do what I call distraction abatement. Get rid of all distractions and hindrances that are not directly helping you (financially speaking, of course; the kids can stay).

Don't be your own worst enemy. The Bible says to "flee from temptation." We need to be extreme at this point. If you can't manage your time to its maximum because of video games or television, then get rid of them. Getting rid of your television and your video games benefits you two fold; you don't waste as much time consumed by them, and you save a lot of money that you would have been spending on cable, or buying video games.

I believe video games are around sixty dollars. That is ridiculous! Get rid of any habits, collections, and other things that hold you back from reaching your full financial potential—unless you are already financially independent, and these *are* your dreams, but probably not.

Highest and Best Use

A real estate appraiser will base their appraisal of a property on what is called the "Highest and Best Use." If a property only has a shed on it but is zoned for a factory that could be making millions of dollars a year, the property will be appraised at a value that assumes that the factory will be built there. The property will be worth whatever the highest and best use of the property could potentially be used for.

We need to make the highest and best use of every moment. At all times, we need to ask ourselves what the best and most profitable use of our time would be.

I wrote this book at many different locations: California, Ohio, Texas, Tennessee, at the airport, at the park, and while I was driving. No matter where you are, there are little pockets of time every single day. What do you do with those brief moments? I always try to think about the best thing that I could be doing at any given moment; I plan ahead, and follow through.

Listening to music while you're driving is not the best use of your time. Instead of listening to the radio which is jam-packed with commercials, listen to audio books, learn a new language, prepare for a promotion, study for a test, get phone calls in, expand your vocabulary—the possibilities are endless.

Successful people don't listen to music in their cars. They are on the phone getting things done or listening to the news. In fact, many rich people don't drive themselves, so that they can be more productive while commuting.

Mind Your Own Business

Catching up with friends is good; stalking your friends on social media is bad. How much time do you spend on social media?

I haven't been on any social media for years. If I need to know something, I'll hear about it in the news. If it doesn't make the news, I don't need to hear about it. If something super interesting happens with someone I know, my wife will tell me. For example, my wife just told me yesterday that our friend's water broke, they didn't make it to the hospital, and her mom had to help her give birth in the back seat of the car. That's the kind of interesting story I'm talking about.

I don't care what you just bought at the store. Some people spend hours a day on social media. I'm not mad at them. I just think that they are throwing away precious time, and I want to help you avoid making the same types of wasteful choices.

Don't Fake It Until You Make It

I began this book describing my past lifestyle living in Hollywood and driving fast cars. That only gives me more authority for this section. I speak from experience.

Never act rich. Do not drive rich people cars if you are not rich. Do not eat out at expensive restaurants, if you are not rich.

You need to take care of your appearance and wear decent clothes, but don't blow money like some rich people do. Save as much as you can and keep investing it.

Even if you are rich, don't act rich. Sam Walton was a billionaire, yet he still drove a beat up old pickup truck and lived in Arkansas.

Most millionaires are in hiding. If you don't believe me, read The Millionaire Next Door by Thomas J. Stanley. No one knows who they are. Once people know that you have money you will be bombarded by all your friends and family for favors. You don't need the distractions, and you will actually be a distraction to other people. They will want what you have and be mad that they can't have it. This is the rule; there are a few exceptions.

It is important for people to think that a business is successful. People want to do business with others who are successful; so there is a sense in which you do want to come off as professional until you make it, but don't fake wealth.

Don't buy things you can't afford. It is that simple.

Care Less about Things That Don't Matter

Why do children fight over who sits in the middle seat in the car? Why do teenagers compare muscles? Why do adults compete with their neighbors to see who has the nicer house, car, etc.? The answer is their pride, but we need to care less about things that don't matter. For example, does it matter what you eat for lunch? No, as long as you have a balanced diet and your body gets the nutrients it needs, you're fine. Does it matter what brand of clothing you wear? It might, but probably not.

Keep your mind fixed on your goals and concern yourself less with the petty things in life that really have no long-term bearing. Yes, the child in the middle seat has a better view of the road, but since they aren't driving, it doesn't matter.

The time you spend on something should be directly correlated to its importance. If you are ordering food at a drive through, just pick something. If you are deciding who you should marry, spend a little more time on that.

Cut Your Losses

Cut your losses. If you see that doing a certain activity isn't going to benefit you greatly...then stop it. Here's an example for the younger readers and the parents of children: if you love basketball, but you are not getting any playing time on the school team because you are just not good enough, then you are probably not going to get a scholarship or become a professional athlete. I would suggest that you not try out next year, and play in a rec. league. You'll have way more time to study and score high on the SAT, thereby getting more scholarship money. Now that's a calculated decision!

If you aren't getting paid for it, or if it won't directly benefit you in the near future financially, it is a distraction. Do something you are good at. Focus on your talents, not weaknesses. By all means, better your weaknesses –if you feel like it; I never did – but don't pursue let's say, a career in your greatest weakness.

Instead, free up your schedule so that you can invest your time in something more profitable.

Redeeming the Time

"Therefore be careful how you walk, not as unwise men but as wise, making the most out of your time, because the days are evil." –Ephesians 5:15-16

You have to take time aggressively. Time doesn't yield itself willingly. You have to actively and intentionally take it. Again, we want to be extreme. Every moment that you can save adds up.

My examples are applicable no matter your age. For me, I was groomed at a young age. As a child, I was applying these lessons and have only grown in my ability to apply them as the decades have passed. When I went to summer camp as a Boy Scout I got as many merit badges as I possibly could. We would sign up for merit badge classes that took place during the day, and maybe we could get four or five merit badges at the camp. I would get seven or eight. In between classes, I would slip into other classes and get those merit badges too. I also competed in all of the games. I did everything I could do to get the most out of that week as possible.

Once, I went to New Orleans for a week to help reconstruct a house that had been destroyed by Hurricane Katrina. The day I got back I went on a road trip with my friends to Chicago to help in the soup kitchen and to volunteer at a camp for disadvantaged youth. Shortly after that I went to the Mexico border to help with a summer camp, then as soon as I got back I went to Germany for a while, a week later I was touring with a band around the nation, then a week later I left the United States to live on a cruise ship for about four months. I could keep going, but you get the point.

Don't settle for normal. Milk every opportunity.

Live like there is no tomorrow.

Carpe Diem is Latin for "Seize the day." The original meaning meant to focus only on today with no regard for the future. I disagree with the latter part of that definition, but the former part is good.

Take full advantage of every opportunity, situation, and circumstance. You better have a good reason to miss a trip, if it is possible for you to go.

Respect for Others' Time

Be mindful of other people's time in the same manner as you are of your own. The billionaire Mark Cuban doesn't even answer his friend's phone calls. He makes them text him. I'm not saying that he is the rule and that you should or shouldn't call others, but maybe shoot them a text first so that they can respond when it is most convenient for them. What I am saying is that however you can save them time, do it.

Try to set out to save both you and others' time. When you are meeting with a friend for coffee, be mindful of how far they have to drive and what their schedule is.

Ask for Directions

Don't be afraid to ask for directions, or where something is in a store. If you don't know right away, ask. This normally saves a lot of time, especially over a long period.

I went into a local auto store in search for A/C refrigerant. None of the aisles seemed to have a name that matched the general genre of product I was looking for. At this point, I asked an employee. Rather than looking through every aisle, I saved myself time by asking. Especially in this instance, since the refrigerant was at the front by the register. Save yourself both time and frustration by being quick to seek the assistance of those that know and can help you find your answer, especially if it's their profession to do so.

You're not wasting their time because they already sold their time to their employer, so it is now the employer's time, but it's still not wasted because I am a paying customer and keeping me satisfied will benefit the company's bottom line.

Multi-Tasking

The multi-tasking principle is a practical way of redeeming your time. Now that I'm married I multi-task differently because she runs the show at home. When I was single, I needed to be very strategic with my time to get more responsibilities done on my own. I would have the washing machine cleaning my clothes while I was downloading something on the computer. At the same time, I was learning the drum parts to music that I needed to play for that night's show. I usually had two to three things happening at one time.

Here are some tips:

-To help you multi-task, place objects in such a way that it takes you less time to reach them.

-Cut the distance down between your activities by organizing your surroundings first.

-Think about how you are going to do your next task while you're doing your present task...but this is not for everyone.

-Do tasks quickly if you can--especially if it's a mundane one and you do it often.

-Incorporate a method that allows you to do a second task that will not have any negative bearing on the one you are currently doing. In other words, kill two birds with one stone.

Minimalism

Marathon Runners would run naked in the Olympics, and so should you—figuratively speaking of course.

The goal of this book is to give you the tools to think bigger and reach your full potential, but first, we need to down-size.

The less you have, the better. The smaller your house is (within reason), the more efficient everything is; the less you have to worry about; and the more freedom you have. This is the concept of minimalism.

How many pairs of shoes do you own? How many articles of clothing do you own? Your answers to these two questions typically reveal how free you are. The goal is freedom. The goal is to have less stress. The goal is to have less time wasted.

At our house, we have books, a lot of books. Having books is great, but you really notice how many books you have when you move to a new home; they are really heavy. Needless to say, we don't have much of anything else. All of our belongings could easily fit in a five hundred square foot apartment. We don't own a television. Needless to say, we don't play video games or have cable. We also don't drive sports cars anymore either. It turns out that the speed limit is the same for everyone, regardless of your horsepower.

There are many great benefits of a minimalist lifestyle. One great benefit is avoiding the rat race. Most people make more and more money, but their lifestyle rises in step with their income.

Dream Big Live Bigger

These people who are stuck in this rat race have a difficult, if not impossible time getting ahead in life. I know people who should be millionaires, but they like to buy nice things. And they like to buy them in abundance, and often. They make over a hundred thousand dollars a year, but can't manage to save up for a house.

You need to simplify everything in your life. Buy or keep a few nice things and then sell what is unnecessary.

Part 3:

KNOWLEDGE

6. THINK ABOUT IT

The third element that you have to cultivate is knowledge. It is third because I believe that wisdom and time are more important. Knowledge can be gained, but it is also forgotten. You can lose it, but you can always get it back—unless you're sick and/or dying.

As Warren Buffett says, the more you learn, the more you earn. Intentional learning of a certain marketable topic is valuable, but if you know more than anyone else about a certain topic, you win. You win the job; you win whatever you were competing for. If you want to win at life, make sure to read this section and apply it to your life.

How Does Sleep Affect Our Bodies?

In order to function at full capacity, make sure you are getting proper sleep.

Can we die from not getting enough sleep?

A 1989 research experiment was conducted on the effects of sleep deprivation. Doctor Allan Rechtschaffen led the experimentation on a group of lab rats. The results of this study were significant in their impact on sleep. All of the lab rats that were deprived of proper sleep died within two to three weeks. Some of the rats in the large group did survive based on the deprivation ceasing prior to two weeks.

These findings helped in the overall case study proving that sleep deprivation has an effect on the overall system. Although it has never been performed on a human, these studies are

73

Dream Big Live Bigger

consistent in their results to show that whether an animal or person, lack of sleep will deteriorate the mind, nerve functions and can cause death.[14]

If you want to be able to learn, then do your brain a favor and get proper sleep—or you might die. Alright, you're probably not going to die, but you get the point.

Mentorship

"A wise man will hear and increase in learning, and a man of understanding will acquire wise counsel"—Proverbs 1:5

Imagine how knowledgeable you would be about investing if Warren Buffett was your mentor. Imagine if Bill Gates helped you learn about computer software. Mentors open up doors; they bring opportunity and teach you things you could never have learned on your own.

We need to be taught how to live our dreams. We can choose to learn from our mistakes, or we can learn from the successes of those who went before us.

Like I did, find a couple with a rags to riches story and spend time with them. Learn from them so that you can do what they did. Find someone who you want to be like and find out what they did to get successful.

> "Your mentors have been to the top of the mountain before. They know the terrain, the challenges, and the pitfalls. Your mentor knows what to do. More important, your mentor knows what NOT to do. They help you avoid lost time and money in trying to correct rookie mistakes. Your mentor also knows the shortcuts, the time-savers,

Think About It

the little tricks. You need a mentor."..."Very few people achieve great success without personal mentors."[15]
—Robert G. Allen, co-author of *The One Minute Millionaire*

When should you change mentors? There are three core factors in deciding if and when it is time to find a new mentor.

One: When you have thoroughly absorbed all that you can from your mentor and reached their plateau. If your mentor decides that they have nothing more to teach you, this may be a helpful indicator.

Two: If you are forced to move long distance, nullifying the life-on-life learning aspect from mentorship.

Three: If a major character flaw is discovered that disqualifies their mentorship. The point of mentorship is learning from someone you want to become like.

Although mentorship is crucial and those who have it excel, ensure that you're still listening to a variety of people. There is wisdom in a multitude of counsel. Don't make the hindering mistake of only listening to someone because of their fame or position in your family. Take it all in. Weigh it all. Discern through it. You might only have one person that you can have life-on-life mentorship with, but make sure you're gaining as much knowledge as possible from as many successful people as possible. You might have one main mentor and a lot of other sub-mentors. Or, you might not have any main mentors. The point is to learn as much as possible from these people that you look up to.

You can be mentored by almost anyone. If they won't come to you and you can't go to them, then pick up a book that they wrote; watch interviews of them.

Mentors leave a legacy. Their students are that legacy.

Ask for Help

Let people know what you are doing, especially if they are in a position to help.

I've traveled the world, and I've learned a great lesson: go with a group, and have someone help you get around. If you are going to New York City, try to get a friend or acquaintance, preferably one that is a resident, to show you around. It is no fun trying to figure your way around by yourself and can often put you into less preferable situations. (I won't get into time wasting.)

I was once traveling with a group from Agra to New Delhi via train. We were getting off the train, and I decided to allow two strangers to go ahead of me, slightly separating me from my group. They were within eye distance, but the two strangers had more luggage than I anticipated. By the time I was able to get off the train, my group was out of sight. I had no way of contacting anyone in my group and I did not know the way back to the hotel. It was the middle of the night, and I was lost in India. I eventually made it back safely. My point is, go with a group and make sure you stay with them. If you don't know what you're doing, you better make sure you are with someone who does.

Ask for help when you need help. You can bet your bottom dollar I asked for help when I was stranded in India. There are many areas of life when it is important to ask for help.

Asking for help is great when looking for a new job. You would be surprised how many people want to help others find a job. Most of the time, they have empathy because they were once in your shoes.

Think About It

If you are moving to somewhere that you have never been before, find a friend or relative that could help. My wife and I moved from Los Angeles to Houston and had no idea where we should live within the city. There are a lot of things to consider: traffic, safety, commute time, etc. I had a friend who already lived in Houston show me a map, explain everything, and help me find different apartments. It saved me a lot of time. Make sure you ask for help.

Be Teachable

"Fools despise wisdom and instruction"—Proverbs 1:7b

"Teachability" is one of those characteristics that tend to be overlooked. When someone is found to have a teachable spirit, people normally ridicule them for it. Take a spousal relationship for example, how often is it mentioned in society that a man is less of a man if he is teachable?

Sometimes women make remarks of a timeframe in which it took them to 'train their husbands.' It is a sad outlook and a skewed one at that. The reality is that everyone needs to learn from and about others. Learn another's personality, what makes them motivated, what provokes them, and what makes them eager or happy. When we stop pretending we already know everything then real learning occurs. This is known as being or possessing a teachable spirit.

Feed this desire to learn. Feed this ability to admit that there is a vast amount of information about others and even your skill set that you can grow in. The more teachable you are, the more able you are to be taught and to advance. Do not be a hard head. Do not push aside learning. It will be to your detriment if you do.

7. TRAINING

Businesses are always investing their resources in developing better products and placing them into the marketplace. We need to invest our resources in ourselves because we are a business, and we (our skills and talents) do provide a marketable service. Whatever your skill set, and whatever you're doing for a job is the service that your company (you) provides. Your company makes income (wages) just like a real company makes income; we just call it by different names. We should always be progressing, just like a business.

Businesses invest their resources in Research and Development. Shouldn't we invest our time and resources to educate and better ourselves, maybe even get better at, or learn a new skill? We should have a plan for the next year; five years from now; ten years from now. Shouldn't we? We need to keep learning, experiencing, and traveling. Just note that there are always temptations competing for your desires and time. We need to be continuously improving ourselves (creating a better service/product).

Always expand your vocabulary. Know the meaning of the words that you use. If you get a consolation prize, you should know what the word "console" means. Whenever you see a word you don't know, always look it up. If you can't look it up right away, write it down on a scrap piece of paper, notebook, your hand, or text it to someone; whatever it takes.

One way to ensure that you are always progressing is by constantly asking yourself "Is there a better way of doing what I'm doing?"

Being Well-Rounded

"Let the wise hear and increase in learning"—Proverbs 1:5

Always progress and always keep bettering yourself. Be the best that you can be at everything.

Sam Walton, the founder of Wal-Mart, was an extremely well-rounded man. He was an Eagle Scout, an athlete, and an entrepreneur. Sam Walton got his private pilot's license and flew around the country planting Wal-Mart stores. Perhaps he knew that to be more efficient, more productive, and more competitive he needed to have the flexibility of flying wherever, whenever, without waiting hours at the airport.

Explore your different interests. The point is to learn everything about something and something about everything. You should be able to walk into a dinner party and hold conversations with people from different socioeconomic groups, thus expanding your network and helping you achieve your goals.

Honing In

The chances are that you won't be the best at everything. You probably weren't the best at every sport, and you probably don't have the same level of skill at all the things you can do. Like most, if not all people, you were created with certain special skills. These are the skills you need to enhance.

One of my special abilities is playing the drums. For most of my life, I have been playing, since the age of six to be exact. I was born with this ability; I didn't ask for it, and I can't change it.

Training

My abilities to play the drums have taken me all over the nation, and I've been a part of various bands. One notable story that would perfectly illustrate my point is when I went on a nationwide tour with an aggressive, alternative rock band.

To make the band, I had to try out, which consisted of me putting together a demo video. I needed to show my knowledge and skills by playing basic rudiments, covering a few songs from different genres, and by showing myself playing in a live show. Then, I had a couple of phone interviews, and I was on my way to Indianapolis. It turns out that I had to beat ten other drummers to win the spot.

Traveling with a director, manager, and five other band members was definitely a growing experience. Every person was from a different state: the lead singer was from Wisconsin, the bass guitar player was from West Virginia, and the other singer was from Texas. There were eight different cultures, eight different personalities, and thousands of miles of being closer than any strangers should be, but it was great.

I had a great time playing shows with great musicians, and I have a lot of great stories to tell.

I was able to have these, among many great experiences, because I polished one skill. You can't do everything. You're only one person; you can't specialize in everything. Maximize your strengths. Invest in your strengths. It's like putting hotels on your most valuable properties in the game of Monopoly. Now apply this principle to your career. Don't try to be the Jack of all trades. You don't want to participate in too many programs and change careers often—unless one job builds upon another, of course. Otherwise, you might appear lost and desperate like you have no idea what you want to do. The faster you figure out your goals, the better. Maximize your strengths. Invest in your strengths. Be really good at a few things. You will find that you do those few things far better than a wider range of activities, and will be more valuable.

Know the Law

Know the law and use your rights to their fullest extent to be more productive. Don't be ignorant of the law. Avoiding tickets, fines, or even worse, will save you a lot of emotional distress, time, and money. Knowing the law also helps you to focus more on being productive because you are not worried about breaking the law.

You *must* know basic tax law. Making a lot of money doesn't make you wealthy; being able to keep that money does. We need to know about taxes, have the biggest write-offs, and pay the least amount of taxes; instead of unnecessarily giving our money to the government out of ignorance.

Going Back to School

The smarter you are, the better people will treat you. Did you know that accountants are treated like kings in Russia? And, if you're bi-lingual, you get better deals in India and Mexico in the markets; just some random facts.

Schooling is important, so here are a few pointers for you to consider.

LIVE NEAR SCHOOLS

Always live where you will have a lot of options to further your education. You might be 45 years old and decide that your best option is to go back to college part time. Education is valuable. You want to give yourself options. Live where there are a few big named, first tier schools, and where there are a lot of community colleges.

At the time that I'm writing this book, there are a lot of online options popping up. You can get your MBA or any other master's degree online. You'll still pay about the same price as if you sat in the actual classroom, but your online degree is usually as good as if you had sat in a classroom. The only drawback is that you won't have the same networking abilities.

Be mindful of the educational resources in a location that you are living in and those of the place you might be moving to. Move somewhere that you can expand your education.

BE HESITANT

However, be extremely hesitant to go back to school. Almost everything you desire to learn can be done via the internet and publically available literature. If you want to learn about finances, geology, or anything else, just pick up a book and start reading.

Only go back to school if it is clear that you have hit a career ceiling, or if you need to go to school to get a certain license. Because it is easier to get a degree, employers are requiring a certain education level to get promoted. This is called *progressive credentialism*. For better or for worse, a college degree is worth less and less because more people have them now. You may run into the career ceiling sooner than you thought and be forced to go back to school to advance. If that happens then you need to be ready.

Another reason to attend graduate school is if you want to become a doctor or any other very specific field necessitating classroom training.

Sometimes it's most strategic to enroll in a class, find out what books that class requires, drop the class, and get the books. Or better yet, just find out what books they use and get them.

If you have to go back to school, avoid going into debt for college, if at all possible. In the recent past, there has been a lot of talk about the college debt bubble with rising prices of tuition; high student loan debt; and low placement rates, but a lot of officials believe that the bubble has burst. At some schools tuition rates have now slowed, and enrollment has gone down. There has never been a better time to get a discount rate on a college degree. Use every strategy to get a great price on your education, and stay out of debt.

I know of a person who quit their job to go to a top law school and a top business school. They couldn't find a job after graduation, and ended up at their old job.

USE THEIR NETWORK

If you are going to go back to school, i.e. get your master's; be intentional to enroll only in a school that is well known for its networking. That is something that is more difficult to get without going to a graduate school.

Training

Again, the networking is nonexistent with online programs, but if all you need is a stamp on your resume, then this could be a great option.

Do Employers Care Where You Went to School?

Most employers ultimately don't care where you went to school, but some employers do work with different universities called feeder schools to help them produce their curriculum. Hence, they know what the students have been learning and what skills they are developing. This doesn't truly happen unless you go to a top tier school.

Some employers do care initially where one got their MBA from, but if you don't produce they will fire you quickly. I know of a handful of people who went to top universities, got into the best investment banks, and made around $125,000 a year. They were also fired soon after being hired. Your employer has to think that you're worth top dollar in order to get the job, but you have to keep producing that value to keep that job.

Theoretically, you would be worth that money if you made it into a top school and graduated, but the pressure never lets up.

When it Matters

One benefit of going to a higher education institution is that some employers don't want potential, they want degrees. They don't know you from Adam, so to reduce the risk of employing a flop they look for a proven record. The record could come from years of business success or graduating top of your class.

You are always a risk to an employer because they are going to invest a lot of time, money, and energy training you. They are losing money on you the first several months of you starting your position. A degree from school shows diligence, competency, and many other qualities that are meant to prove that you aren't a high risk to potential employers.

Go to school if you need it to get a license. Many options are more affordable than a master's degree and set you up to begin your career within a year. Trade schools and working certifications are some of the best outlets for getting a return on your investment. Cosmetology school or welding schools are two examples among many. You can get your C.P.A. license without ever possessing an actual master's degree. The credits required to sit for your exam can even be done at some community colleges.

HOW TO PICK THE SCHOOL

Look for schools that offer the major that you are interested in. Most people don't have a problem doing that.

Next--and this is very important--look for their accreditation. Are they accredited? By who are they accredited? Is there a school nearby that offers the same degrees with a higher accreditation?

Think about it. There is a reason one school is accredited higher than the other. Learn the criteria it takes for a school to earn the highest accreditation. More experienced faculty? Higher selectivity?

Some employers are totally ignorant of your college's accreditation, but graduate schools are not, and there are a lot of employers who are fully aware of the different accreditations

Training

and partner with those schools. These employers will actively hire from the highest accredited schools, and these are the well-established employers that you want to work for.

Ask Tons of Questions

If knowledge is power, which it is, then ask a million questions. Just be sure to read your audience and don't ask inappropriate questions for the situation. Every employer, supervisor, teacher, and instructor should know you by name (but not for negative reasons). Your employer should know your name based on your excellent performance and desire to know more about how to serve the company. There will be the few that become annoyed by your desire for knowledge, but that's not necessarily a bad thing. Most teachers will not be annoyed, but even if they are...you are paying them to answer your questions. Your classmates might be annoyed, but those who are success bound will respect and look up to you. Of course, the honor comes only if you ask intelligent and relevant questions. Don't be ridiculous or inconsiderate.

Whenever Warren Buffett speaks, he will normally do a Q and A, with only a brief introductory lecture.

If successful people know that questions are beneficial, then why is it that we stop asking them? In a recent study, it was brought to light how many questions children ask per day. Four-year-old girls are the most curious, asking an incredible 390 questions per day. At the other end of the spectrum, nine-year-old boys are more content with their knowledge, asking 144 questions per day. Why did the questions decrease? [16]

What do children have that adults don't: unlimited dreams, unrestricted ambition, and unrestrained imaginations? Children don't know that they can't do something until someone tells them that they can't. Someone or something has to steal their ambition away from them.

Training

For the most part, the questions that children ask revolve around what they aspire to be when they grow up. If the child dreams of being an astronaut, their questions will be about space. How do I become an astronaut? How many stars are in the sky? How far away is the moon? They aren't asking questions about what they don't care about.

Again, we need to reclaim these lost ambitions. The frequency of our questions and the types of questions that we ask reveal how ambitious we are. Begin to ask bigger questions and more of them.

Most answers are preceded by a question. The question is either asked in your thoughts, or to someone who you think might know the answer. Logically, the more questions you ask, the more knowledge you will obtain.

Some say "a little knowledge is dangerous," but we don't want a little knowledge. We want to blow the competition away by mastering subjects.

Field Trips

Traveling is a great way to learn. Think of traveling as a field trip; be it locally or to a different area. Soak in the whole experience.

I have traveled a lot and learned from every trip. I know details about the Khmer Rouge regime that not many know. I've seen the tower with a display of skulls piled inside of it; a tower built on the killing fields in Cambodia where thousands were taken to be buried. Most individuals have never heard of the Khmer Rouge Regime at all.

Dream Big Live Bigger

I will never forget the Vietnam War. This is not because I fought while the war was happening, but because I've been in the Cu Chi underground tunnel system designed to allow the Viet Kong to ambush the American troops. I have seen the sick and morbid booby traps set up by the Viet Kong.

I will never forget all the chemical weapons used to destroy the Vietnam trail, and seeing all the deformed faces of those victims begging me for money.

I've seen the desperately poor Capoeira performers in Brazil asking for money after they performed in the streets and getting yelled at if I didn't give them money.

I know about the Apartheid in Cape Town, South Africa. Not because I was taught about this in school –I wasn't. I know because I was there.

I've had dinner in the Eiffel Tower, and I've seen the riots after a soccer match, regardless of who won.

I know the smells; I've seen the sites.

I knew a lot more about the world in my early twenties than most will learn in their entire lives. Not to sound like I'm boasting; it's just a sobering fact. Traveling catapults your education, and it changes the way you think and live.

Travel as much as you can, but with purpose. It will open your eyes to possibilities, and you will dream big and live bigger than you ever have.

Travel as much as you can, then never go back. The next time you travel, try to go to a place you've never been to before. The world is big enough, and there is enough to learn and experience that you should try going to a different place on your next trip.

Training

I was speaking to an audience about some of my trips, and I was asked if I would go on any of them again. I thought about it for a few seconds, but only a few seconds; the answer was no.

Movies

"I learn a lot from movies" – Jack Ma, founder of Alibaba

You can learn through a lot of different avenues; movies are one of them. If you're watching movies for a real educational purpose, then you won't need to watch them again—unless you feel that you didn't retain all the information the first time. Maybe even bring a notepad to write terms you've never heard before so that you can look them up later.

Debrief after a movie with someone to discuss what was learned, applies to you, and could benefit you. Or talk about what you didn't like, so you know what not to do also. Keep your mind practiced in discernment and being an active thinker.

Be an active watcher, just like you would be an active reader. Active readers engage with the book. They even argue with the writer and will write thoughts in the margins. Do the same with watching a movie.

8. CALCULATED DECISIONS

How do we make decisions? On the surface level, we will use the phrase calculated decisions. Though, we will discuss this on a deeper level later in the book.

The word decision means to *cut off*. When you choose one thing, you cut away the other options. We need to begin to cut away all bad habits and poor decisions.

My friend who owned his own business knew the importance of calculated decisions. He would go out to eat knowing that he was getting a better deal than if he had to cook the steak himself. He would always say, "It would have cost me way more to drive to the grocery store, park, shop for the meat, wait in line to pay for the meat, buy the sides (green beans, etc.), drive home, cook, prepare all the food, then clean up... I could never have gotten this meal for a lower price." He could have been working and making more money during that time. And he's single. He made more money than he would be spending during that time frame. He made a calculated decision.

That same friend taught me how to buy a plane ticket for twenty dollars to fly from Houston, Texas to LAX. That might have been a one-way ticket, but that's still cheap. We did this by taking advantage of a membership program and by buying the tickets at the airport. My point is that every action can be intentional and calculated.

Every mom that is cutting coupons so that she can meet their tight budget is making a calculated decision. Every dad that stays late at work, or works over time is making a calculated decision.

In a sense, everyone makes calculated decisions. We all pick the shortest lines at McDonald's, but sadly most make bad calculations. This happens mostly with how we spend our time, what we feed ourselves, and what we spend our money on. Hopefully, this book will help with these habits.

Not every decision will guarantee success because we will never be able to have perfect information, and things always change. There will always be an element of risk because we make decisions with information and resources that you currently don't have.

Make most of your risky decisions while you are young and before you have a spouse or children. If you make a risky decision, and it was a mistake, you don't want to take your closest loved ones with you as you fall.

If you are single, pack up your bags and make that ridiculous move to a place you've always dreamed about. Live where you want to live. Now is the time. Once you start a family, your options will narrow.

There is a well-known expression, "my mind's made up, so don't confuse me with facts." Most people who make bad decisions are stubborn, hard-headed, and obstinate. They won't listen to anyone, and you can't change their mind by giving them new information. This mind-frame will devastate your future and stop you from reaching your full potential.

Don't Rely on Signs

My friends and I were invited to speak at a church. The pastor of the church admitted in front of the entire audience that he chose to have us speak because he saw an advertisement on the side of a semi-truck with the name of our college on it. My jaw dropped when I heard him say that.

Calculated Decisions

Don't make decisions based on a 'sign.' A sign could be a billboard, a song that is being played on the radio, or anything of that nature. To make decisions based off of so-called signs is to jump head first into a shallow river not knowing what rocks sit beneath the surface. It is jumping on a whim because you 'felt' a pull. I urge you to make decisions based upon reason, logic, and truth.

There should be a good amount of logical information in favor of a decision before making a large leap. Maybe there are bits of information missing, and you decide to move forward, but your foundation is there. Living for signs is what I would like to call 'blind faith.' You are putting more faith in a sign than in a logical, calculated decision.

You *know* whether a decision is reasonable or if it's a hasty, "feelings" driven one. No one needs to tell you unless you're lying to yourself; in which case you have to ask for counsel. Don't rely on your emotions or signs to make decisions.

Whenever you're making a decision, ask yourself if it is logical... and ask others if it's logical. You should literally ask them that question.

Play the Cards in Your Hands

Life is often about being strategic.

There are a lot of board games that require strategy. I urge you to become familiar with the concepts that may be derived from these games. In short, I will share a principle that relates to my point. The cards you have been dealt are the cards you have to strategize with. You might pick up different cards on your next turn, but you can't make decisions based on cards you don't have.

Weighing your options and statistics of how long it would take to obtain the needed cards versus using what you have is part of the strategy. If you wait too long on a goal that you are dead set on, you may miss your opportunity. Instead, create your opportunities by being willing to change course. Sometimes a road less traveled is what it takes to get to your goal sooner. It may not be the popular action in the game or life, but it is a surer plan than waiting on hopes.

You are handed a certain set of cards to play in life. Part of building your strategy is to know when to use your cards and how many at any given time. Play the cards that you have in your hand, and learn the best possible way to play them. This means that you don't wait to pick up more options/cards, not knowing if it will pan out the way you are hoping.

Don't spend money you don't have and don't promise time you can't give.

You may not like everything about the particular situation that you are in, but there is always an advantage to that situation. Learn how to take full advantage of the benefits inherent in every situation. This is particular useful in the context of your job.

Recognize the cards that you have, and learn how to play them so that you can have the absolute best results.

Being Risk Averse

Never take unnecessary risks. Be as risk averse as possible. There will always be risk involved in any decision, but don't make unnecessary risks. Unnecessary risks include gambling or moving to a new state or country without a good plan. Be risk averse because one big mistake is very difficult to bounce back from.

Your educated strategies will include a small risk that you can base your calculated decision on. Perhaps you got a job offer in a different state, so you decide to move to take that job. That sounds logical. Things might not work out and you might get fired after only working there for a month or two, but that is still a solid decision.

We are very much out of control. We don't and can't control very much, but you can minimize your risk.

The Tragedy of the Commons

When making calculated decisions that involve multiple people, you must understand the principle of The Tragedy of the Commons. We know that everyone always acts in what they believe to be their best interest, but this rule directly clashes when you are sharing resources. If someone is looking out for their best interest, they are not looking out for the interest of the group.

This principle is most obvious in a bachelor pad. The rule of the Tragedy of the Commons says that messiest rooms in the house will be the living room, the kitchen, and the bathrooms; any room that is shared. The reason is that it is in the individuals' best interest to not clean and leave it for someone else to clean.

The workplace break room is another example of such. It is especially frustrating for the individual that ends up cleaning up after everyone else.

A third example is sharing limited resources. If you give four children a bowl of candy with no restrictions, they will race to the bowl, and the person who gets there first will take all the candy while fighting off the other three children. It is in the individuals' best interest to take all of the candy; regardless of fairness, and a total disregard of logic. Even if the child doesn't plan on eating all the candy at that moment, they will still take as much as they physically can and hide what they don't want to eat at that moment.

How does this affect our decision making? Let me suggest not sharing any resources or common areas with people. Be as autonomous as you can. Actively put yourself in a position to have your own things. Set yourself up in a way that, even if you do happen to share something, you have no desperate need to run to the candy bowl.

Quiet Time

Give yourself quiet time to think. Every big decision needs to be preceded by a lot of thinking. This principle compliments other principles in this book like, taking a longer amount of time to decide when it is an important decision.

Not all decisions will require quiet time to think, but when one does, go to a place with no distractions, especially emotional ones. There doesn't need to be one special place to do your thinking. It could be driving, showering, or lying in bed. The hardest part of doing this is getting rid of a distraction, hence the word *quiet*.

Quiet thinking enables you to sort out and organize the information you have. It allows you to wrestle through your resources and strategize without the interruptions of everyday life and distractions.

Part 4:

MONEY

9. LIVE LONG AND PROSPER

What is money? What is marketing? Why should I care about earning money?

Not all success is measured in dollars. The mom, who guides her children faithfully until they create their own stories, is successful. I don't want you to believe that I am defining success by how much wealth you have—because I'm not.

The fact is that most dreams *do* involve money. Some people dream about giving away a lot of money, and some dream about having a lot of it, but all dreams, in one way or another typically involve money. Part four of this book will address principles of money that you must understand to live out your dream.

Bringing Value to Society

According to the dictionary, money is "any circulating medium of exchange."[17]Money includes gold, silver, bitcoins, and anything else that others are willing to exchange for goods and services. I will be using this definition when I refer to money throughout this part.

The principle behind getting money is simple; if you bring value to society, you will get paid. It is as simple as that. To get money, you must provide value. If you don't provide value, you won't get a dime—unless you find one on the street.

Even panhandlers on the street corners bring some type of infinitesimal value to society. We would not give them money unless it made us feel good to do so. I understand that a few exceptions come to mind, but try to stay with me. These are the basic principles of money.

Bring everyone around you as much value as you can. You never know who will become an indispensable contact. In any conversation, the more value you bring to the table in the form of information, the more value you will get out of the conversation, maybe in the form of respect, or some other form, but it'll still be there.

What is the Market?

The word *market* means the same thing as it always has. In older times people had to go to the farmers market to buy food. You bring your product to sell at the market, just like big corporations bring their products to the market. You buy products at the market with the same concepts as people living in the eighteenth century did. If you are in the market, that means you are either there to buy or sell something.

Money is Amoral

Money is a tool. It is not inherently good or evil. Money has no morals.

One of my mentors told me that I should live off of around forty thousand a year and give the rest away to help other people, regardless of how much I was making a year. I could be a doctor making hundreds of thousands of dollars, but I could only live off of forty thousand a year.

I understand the heart behind it, helping others is good, but those who do give so much away need to be careful that they aren't legalistic. We can cross the line and think that having money is bad and that we *must* give a certain amount away.

Rich people are not better or worse than poor people. Having money doesn't make you a bad person, and having little doesn't make you a good one either. Money is amoral.

Help Others Live Their Dream

When some of my family came to visit me for their first time in Los Angeles they had a few requests. One, they wanted to see the Hollywood sign. Two, they wanted to see the Pacific Ocean. It had been a lifelong dream for my grandmother to put her feet in the Pacific Ocean, so I made sure we made it to the beach. Once we finally made it to the beach, there was a child-like smile on her face.

My mom and I were testing the strength of a starfish by seeing if we could pull it off of a rock when I noticed that my grandma was no longer standing with us. She was already in the water looking down at the sand as she was sinking her feet in it. The waves were splashing against her ankles as she was enjoying the breeze. I don't think I had ever seen her so happy before. Living big helps others fulfill their dreams.

Poor People Can't Help Poor People

Because of their success, Charlie and Sandy were able to give back. Sandy helped found two non-profit organizations that help abused and neglected children. Charlie was the President of the library board which helped to build a new library in his city, among many other philanthropic adventures.

In contrast to this example, I have worked with people who are desperately poor with very little hope of making any dreams come true. Some employees that I worked with didn't have enough gas money to make it home, some were losing their homes, and some had no money for food. To make their ends meet they needed to get check advances. They had made a series of decisions that put themselves in that situation. You can't help *other* people if *you* need help to meet your basic needs. Helping others is a lot easier if you have money.

Happiness

"I was always thinking about getting enough knowledge so that I could get a job that I was happy with."—Charlie Baum

What is happiness? Does money make you happy? Happiness is a direct result of something good that just happened. Happiness depends on happenstance. Money does momentarily put a smile on your face and excitement in your bones. Money doesn't bring you true, long-lasting joy, but it does make you happy.

Happiness is not bad to pursue. Money is the fuel for flexibility. It gives you choices and it gives you options.

Life's Challenges

Money allows you to fight the battles that life brings.

Did you know that the patients in Filipino hospitals have to pay all of their hospital bills before the hospital releases them? You need to have money saved for emergencies.

Later in life, Charlie had to battle cancer. He didn't know how many years he had left. Some of his friends with the same type of cancer didn't survive. Because he was financially prepared, Charlie and Sandy were victors. And because he survived Charlie bought a Corvette with the license plate that says, "To Live."

Their financial success didn't only allow them to buy fancy bottled water and help other people. They also were financially prepared to face life's challenges.

To Charlie and Sandy, being financially successful was not optional. Money represented survival. Not luxury, but life or death.

The Snowball Effect

The more time, money, and knowledge you obtain, the more that possibilities can become a reality. The more goals you reach, the more financial and emotional fuel is added to your next accomplishment until there is a snowball effect and you reach higher and higher goals; and so on. If you follow the instructions in this book, you will quickly see that time, money, and knowledge are not as elusive as most believe.

The amazing fact of life is that ten thousand dollars is easier to save for once you have saved five thousand, and not just because you are halfway there. You will save ten thousand dollars in a fraction of the time that it took you to save five thousand. This is because of the snowball effect.

It takes more effort to start the snowball and get it started moving down the hill than the entire process altogether. Once the snowball is started, all you have to do is guide the snowball as it picks up more and more snow.

The same is true with finances. In the beginning of living on your own, five thousand dollars might be difficult to save up for. Then, in a few months or a few years of following the instructions in this book, five thousand doesn't seem to be that unattainable. You can then invest that five thousand in various ways to help you reach ten thousand dollars.

Maybe you bought a car for $5,000 which helped you get that job that paid more money. Or perhaps having five thousand dollars helped you get through an emergency that would have put you in debt. You get the point. Money is exponentially multiplied when handled correctly.

At first, it is difficult to gain financial traction in life. You will start out making very little. You won't get to pick and choose where you work or how far away from work you live, and you might not have a master's degree and multiple years of experience under your belt. But as you'll see in the following chapters, it is possible to use the snowball effect to one day demand your salary, choose who you work with, and freely decide how far away from work you live.

Materialism

Having money is okay, but being materialistic is not. Possessing money does not necessitate love for material goods. In fact, there is much more that can be done through investing than can be done by merely spending every penny on nice junk.

Materialism is a drive to possess certain tangible things. To a materialistic person, money is a poison. Materialism says: I need more, I need bigger, and it needs to be expensive. Granted, you can be materialistic and yet be a thrift shopper. You don't have to buy the most pristine or name brand items to have your heart completely wrapped up in a love for stuff. Check your heart. When you are done, check it again.

Paycheck to Paycheck

One goal of mine was to get to a point when we could say "how much do we *want* to spend," instead of "how much *can* we spend."

It would shock you if you knew how many people that you thought had their lives' together actually didn't. Most people living on planet Earth are living paycheck to paycheck, and they have to wait until their next paycheck before they *can* buy groceries. Let's say that this example doesn't apply because you have enough for groceries, but if you are renter, can you make your rent payment ahead of time out of your savings?

Those who ask *how much can I buy* are not asking because they are checking their budgets and want to see how much they have left in that specific category. They usually have no emergency fund, no savings, and close to no money at all in the bank.

You might want to take a lower paying part-time job so that you can go back to school. You won't have that option if you are living paycheck to paycheck with no savings.

If you are stuck asking *how much can I spend...*there is hope. Save now and prepay for your future. You don't want to be owned by work the rest of your life.

10. LIVE LIKE YOU'RE ALIVE

"A little sleep, a little slumber, a little folding of the hands to rest, and poverty will come upon you like a robber, and want like an armed man."—Proverbs 6:10-11

Time is fast. We need to be faster. Do things with a purpose. Walk with intentionality. Move like you have a place to go because if you follow the steps in the rest of the book, you *will* have places to go. For at least eight hours a day have a sense of urgency; a sense of purpose.

If you are not proactive, you will not progress in any way, it is called arrested development. You want to develop, but if you're not proactive you will stop your development. You can actually be "younger" than you look, mentally and situationally. We all know adults who are older, but they are in the exact same situation as they were in when they were twenty.

One result of being passive is known as failure to launch. These are the thirty and forty-year-old children who still live in their parent's house. Another result is being a boomerang. These are children who leave the house, mismanage their money, and move back in it like a boomerang. You need to make something of yourself. Have you ever heard someone making the comment, "that person really made something of themselves?" Or, "They never amounted to anything." Let the former be said about you, not the latter.

Money flows to those who are proactive and flees from those who are passive.

Being proactive is not a choice for the top 1% of the richest people. You cannot make it to the top of a mountain without climbing. Nothing else matters if you are not proactive. You must take action.

To save money on your utility bills, take shorter showers. Drink water instead of juice. Get rid of your television. We need to be radical.

You can't control a lot of things in life but those things that you can control, take control of them.

Shoot for the Stars

"Shoot for the stars. If you miss, at least you'll land on the moon." –Anonymous

Maybe you already have goals, but chances are you have put a ceiling on your potential. There is a measure of success that we believe that we can obtain, but past that point is only "impossibility."

You settle for what you think you deserve, and well, you get what you settle for.

We set goals based on what we believe that we can achieve. That's true of everyone. But what we believe we can achieve is vastly different from what we actually can achieve.

There should be reality behind our goals. Most of us will not be making trillions of dollars in the next two weeks. But also don't aim too low. You *can* break that habit! You *can* invent something! You *can* see the world!

Focus

"Wherever you are, be all there." –Jim Elliott

We need to clear our minds of all distractions so that we can focus.

At a small event that I hosted, there was a wealthy man, who was a running back for the Cleveland Browns. Before leaving, he wanted to give me a piece of advice that helped him along his journey. He took both his hands and placed them flat against the sides of his temple. Speaking to me, he directed his hands toward me as if I was the only one who had his attention. His gestures illustrated his words as he told me, "remember…focus."

I love how impacting it was for me. Especially how concise he was in his articulation which indicated that he lived out his advice. He knew how important focusing was, if anyone did. As a running back there were countless distracters around him on and off the field, but he made it his mission to not be engulfed by any of them.

Focusing was one of the most important skills that helped him gain wealth, keep it, and live out his dream of playing in the NFL. The ability to focus is an aspect of self-discipline that allows you to make forward steps toward your dreams. Self-discipline is very much an active step in creating the canvas for focusing. If you are not in the habit of training your mind to ignore outside influences, then you will struggle that much more to fight them. However, self-discipline is only as strong as the self-control that is manifested in the practice of training your mind into a routine. The mind will always want to wander, but it is your obligation to keep yourself on track.

Dream Big Live Bigger

Putting blinders on a horse keeps the horse from going sideways. The horse will walk in a straight line to accomplish its goal. It is not distracted by anything else.

Like I have expounded on elsewhere, distractions take away from your focus. Without a clear direction, hindrances and encumbrances will weigh too heavily. Mental weights will become a problem because it leads to becoming overwhelmed.

You don't want to hit the point of becoming overwhelmed because often this is where people fall the hardest and sometimes don't get back up. For this reason, it is important to be on the alert and safeguard yourself with practical applications of self-control, self-discipline, and clear insight on where it is you are determining to go. Which leads us to another means of avoiding being overwhelmed and maintaining focus: being proactive.

Moving with Intentionality

Do things with a purpose. Walk with intentionality. Move like you have a place to go, because if you follow the steps in the rest of the book you will have places to go.

Take Regular Breaks

Take breaks often. Your brain is not a muscle, but it acts like one because it can be developed. It is a use it or lose it kind of thing.

The brain is made up of billions of tiny nerve cells, called neurons.

"Communication between these brain cells is what allows us to think and solve problems. When you learn new things, these tiny connections in the brain actually multiply and get stronger. The more that you challenge your mind to learn, the more your brain cells grow. Then, things that you once found very hard or even impossible to do—like speaking a foreign language or doing algebra— seem to become easy. The result is a stronger, smarter brain."[18]

You should take breaks from learning, but make your breaks productive.

Make sure you are doing something else on your break, don't just waste time. Most of the time, you just need a break from what you are doing, so keep doing something productive at all times. Take a power nap if that is what will be most conducive to you getting things done after your break. Just don't get carried away with this one.

Working Ahead

If you work ahead and get your obligatory tasks done in advance, you give yourself needed flexibility. If you have a doctor's appointment you can leave your job or school and make your appointment without any negative consequences.

I went to college during high school which gave me the flexibility to finish college in four years and go on all of my adventures.

I lived with a man who actually was able to finish all of his accredited hours for college by the age of eighteen. He was starting his master's degree at the same time most people were starting their bachelor's degree. Now that is working ahead!

113

11. THE FIRST STEP

Keep everything clean and organized.

The very first step to getting things done is to clean up and get organized. Organization is the foundation. You can't build the framing and put the roof on until you have the foundation laid.

Getting organized and keeping things clean will give you peace of mind, which allows you to be more productive. It also makes you more efficient. This creates another snowball effect.

At Work: Clear off your desk of everything, except those things that immediately pertain to what you are doing.

At Home: Clean everything and organize the area before doing your at-home work. Keep your home organized using labels and bins, filing cabinets and whatever else helps you meet your daily tasks.

Get Into a Routine

Get into a routine. This helps you stay organized and helps keep you from forgetting things.

If you are someone who has a difficult time creating your own routine or structure, then this is going to be a task that is all the more important and pertinent to you. You need to have structure. All good things come with structure. I have never in my life heard someone say that having a routine or structure was a poor decision. You and I both know it is part of setting a foundation and a crucial component in the race for time.

Downfalls of not creating order are not being able to strategize as effectively, forgetfulness, and being overall less efficient. Just like any skill, you do something the same way over and over again and you will get really good at it. Getting into a routine will allow you to save time by being quick at each task at hand. Having structure allows you to fit in events or alter your schedule accordingly, knowing ahead of time what you will be busy with each day and at which hours.

Some people are not only self-starters but routine lovers. These people create order from chaos, no matter where they go. However, there are, like I stated, those who seem to do quite the opposite. These are the individuals that perhaps create chaos wherever they go. They live in disorganization and sleep until noon. Habits like these need to be weeded out so that structure can be formed.

If you are the type of person who doesn't fair well with creating order, go the extra step and involve yourself in something that forces a routine upon you. Commit to a morning spin class that requires you to wake early and get your blood pumping. Commit to something that will counteract with your weakest area that is preventing you from maintaining routine in your day. Maybe you will need to call on an outside source for your accountability. I know several couples that ask their spouse's to be their alarm clock or their afternoon check-up to see how they are managing their time. You need to do what it takes to progress forward.

If you want to be your own boss, you will need to be a self-starting, routine oriented individual. Make the initial steps and you will see that it is quite possible. (However, you will need to want it.)

Perhaps you are someone who just does better as an employee rather than being your own boss. (It's not wrong to desire this. Perhaps that is the ultimate order that will drive you to your dream.) Whatever the case, you know if you can create order or not. There is no good excuse for not helping yourself to get on track for the future.

Always Progressing

Progression is a key component to success and the accomplishment of reaching your fullest potential. Be in the mindset that you should always be progressing. No matter what stands in front of you, keep making actions toward your goals. This goes for every goal: short, small and long-term.

Take this example:

If you have a set move out date, begin the process of packing well ahead of time. Start with the little procedures like creating an organized list of what can be packed up first. Schedule each day with what items will be packed up; following the list with what items you will least need. Then pack the ones that will have to wait until the week before you move out. Set aside the crucial items for the last week. Then begin the next day by packing. Take your time to clean, properly wrap, and pack each item. Please don't take more than the necessary amount of time—but maybe the move is emotional so it will take longer the first day or two as you deal with the feelings involved.

Each day as you progress toward your goal of moving, you will begin to notice that this routine you have started is now coming in quite handy. Packing is now extremely organized and quick. You went from not wanting to pack, not being good at packing, and barely beginning the process...to quick, efficient and almost done. Keep progressing always. Even with the harder things in life.

Progress keeps you from idleness. Progress keeps you from discouragement. Progress keeps you from growing weary. Progress keeps you from boredom.

For the Long Haul

Success is predicated on a series of choices. Begin to make a series of decisions that lead you to success. The good news is that you already have by picking up this book.

Make a series of decisions that will help you live the fullest life in the long run, not just in the short-term. A high school star athlete was playing volleyball on the beach. I asked him how he was doing, and he said, "Living the dream." Fast forward a decade and he is probably working in a factory. Don't dream small. Don't plan only for the here and now. Think long-term.

Always have a plan. Have a five to ten-year plan. And if you're really feeling bold, have an eleven-year plan. I always had an eleven-year plan. Why an eleven-year plan? I have no idea; it is just how that one worked out. My point is, at minimum have a five-year plan. A business plan that involves investors and a model for success always is at minimum a five-year plan. Why would anyone invest in your company if you don't have a set-out plan of action for the next five years? The five-year plan is one of the most frequently asked questions in a job interview. Businesses believe having a five-year plan as important. Shouldn't you see the importance in having one too?

This entails that you are making invested decisions for the future. Long-term plans are important because they set you apart from every individual that is living for the moment. Long-term plans show a sense of ambition and commitment while encouraging yourself to aim far in the distance. Keep in mind, the

The First Step

target that is fifty feet away is going to be more challenging than that of ten feet.

I can't begin to describe how having long-term planning has helped me achieve my goals.

"You've got to think about big things while you're doing small things, so that all the small things go in the right direction." –Alvin Toffler, journalist and author

Try to have a backup plan as well. You should never put all your eggs in one basket. My wife and I once placed too much weight in a decision that dealt with us moving. We assumed that I was going to get a job, but we had no firm contract; I didn't have the job yet. Well, we emotionally invested ourselves and others into this plan and when it fell through the damage was done. We had backup plans that allowed us to be fine financially and able to relocate, but the emotional damage was less reversible. We ended up relocating and moving to an entirely different state than we had planned on initially.

To have multiple backup plans is entirely helpful because plans are not absolutes.

This principle goes for job security in more than one way. It can be applied to switching jobs, or to the family man holding a secured position in his company for over twenty-five years. I know a man who fits this last example. He was with his company for close to thirty years when half of the company was laid off. Instead of hiring all those employees back on, the company hired on a new set of employees possessing the most current education in the field. My friend did not foresee that he would lose his, what seemed to be secure, position. Thankfully he had a long-term backup plan that allowed for him to take the necessary next steps for provision for his family.

Of course, plans always change with new and better information, so you don't want to dwell on the future, but we need to do our part to plan ahead.

"The mind of man plans his way, but the LORD directs his steps." –Proverbs 16:9

Maintaining a To-Do List

"The ability to concentrate and to use your time well is everything"—Lee Iacocca, former Ford Motor Company President, and Chrysler Chairman

Hyperthymesia is the ability to memorize everything about one's own life. It has been said that only about twelve people in the world have this ability. Eidetic Memory is a having a photographic memory. Stephen Wiltshire would take a mental photograph of landscapes and architecture, and then draw it from memory. I had a buddy who memorized the entire map of the Los Angeles County. People would call him for directions when they were lost.

Maybe you have a perfect memory; probably not. So, for the 99.9999 percentage of people that don't, make sure you write everything down. If you do not write it down, assume that you will forget it.

We need to have a to-do list. We need to get our thoughts out of our heads and in some kind of software program or a piece of paper. I use One-Note. Most business executives even have personal assistants to remind them of their to-do list. To-do lists help you strategize and prioritize.

So lest you forget my point, write it down.
Don't rely on your memory to do the trick. At some point when you are applying all the lessons of this book, you will realize that

your mind is too occupied to remember the small things. The small things are still important. Write it down.

If you don't write down your ideas and you decide to wait to do it later, then you are voluntarily giving them up. You are knowingly taking the risk that you will forget it. When you free your mind from the task of memorizing, you can use that brain capacity for more productive things.

Don't Wait

Patience is a virtue, waiting is not. Plan proactively so that you are never waiting. If you do find yourself waiting, e.g. you are at the airport waiting because your flight was delayed, and you were not proactive enough to check your emails for possible flight changes, always bring something to do. When you are working on something while you are waiting then it is no longer waiting. You have simply changed the order in which you accomplish tasks.

Don't Procrastinate

Procrastination will make you lose out on opportunities. I trained for seven months for the Flying Pig Marathon in Columbus, Ohio. I even had a special training program that I did with my buddy. We ran through knee deep snow and bone-piercing, cold wind. As the race date drew near I went online to register, but I was too late. The race had been capped at a certain number of participants, and they had closed the registration.

My training partner registered way ahead of time. He got to run the marathon, and he even qualified to run at the Boston Marathon. Logically speaking, I could have qualified for the Boston Marathon! What a blunder on my part.

Dream Big Live Bigger

When it comes to procrastination, most live by one motto, 'Hard work pays off later, procrastination pays off now.' That phrase is sadly a way of life for too many people. The lives' of these people will be stunted, and they will miss out on great experiences in life.

Get things done as soon as they occur if you have the means to. Make it a goal to have the means to, even if you have to get creative; strategizing to produce the time now by shifting (in your mind) plans for later. If you cook dinner, wash the dishes after eating. Don't stack them in the sink (mold can grow, and a full sink means using more counter space, which could cause more cleanup). I'm not trying to boss you around. I'm just explaining a principle.

A business with a stack of accumulated paperwork is putting themselves in danger of getting behind, missing tax deadlines, and having delayed financial reporting. The point is, get things done as you can to save time in the long run.

Not procrastinating gives you an incredible advantage over almost every other human being. You will be surprised how much farther you will get in life, especially in the long run. For example, the average person won't leave their house until the very last minute. When all these procrastinators drive on the freeway, you get stop-and-go traffic. Those who woke up earlier, miss the traffic, get better gas mileage, get more work done, are less likely to be late, are less likely to get fired, and have more time at work to get things done. They are also less stressed out and get fewer speeding tickets. So don't procrastinate.

Procrastination hinders you from being on top of work responsibilities. When you are on top of your work you can have a fuller picture of what's going on in the company and you can find solutions to problems that are normally outside of your typical duties. Perhaps you can help solve an issue at the management level, which will give you a better chance of getting a raise.

Building Confidence

The small victories in life give you confidence for the next goal. When you accomplish the next goal it gives you more confidence for the one after that. This creates another snowball effect. Building confidence is more about facing your fears rather than becoming prideful.

I was recently a guest speaker at a Boy Scout event, and I spoke about building confidence. I asked how many of them would be able to stand in the front and begin speaking. A few raised their hands with a big smile on their faces, so I think they were being silly. I went on to explain how the courage to stand in front of strangers and communicate something meaningful takes a lot of practice. It takes a series of small good speeches and leadership experiences.

A small speech introduces you to public speaking. Then, instead of reverting back to your original confidence level, you build upon the courage that you just gained. The snowball just continues to build after every experience until you can speak on national television in front of millions of viewers. Gaining confidence in these particular skills is absolutely crucial to living out your full potential.

Public speaking is just an example, but it is 75% of leadership, and will open doors and networks that you never had access to. This is especially true if you are a motivational speaker.

There is something very unique and real about how excitement has the tendency to directly motivate. Knowing this, employers appreciate and reward people who can motivate others. Bosses try to evoke excitement in their employees for the work they do. Accomplishments and work well-done ignite this type of passion for the continuation of that job or skill.

Don't Get Puffed Up

If you read and apply the principles in this book you will accelerate your life, but you need to be careful. When some people start to gain wealth and success, they get puffed up and they lose it all. They become too prideful. They think they are too good for others. Money is not the distinguisher of: good or bad, ethically correct or immoral, or classy or trashy.

Don't forget that wealth does not set you above anyone any more than your race or gender does. Each is only a characteristic that you possess that perhaps makes you different but does not equate to favor. You are still on the same level as others; you are still in the same position of setting goals, seeking wisdom, seeking knowledge and aiming to use your time discerningly. Lest you lose sight of these, remind yourself that money does not make you better; it merely makes you responsible for more.

12. HOW TO CHOOSE A CAREER

What do you want to be when you grow up? You've probably been asked that before. I suggest that you become who you want to be now. It's never too late to become who you want to be, regardless of your age.

You should choose what you want to do with your life because you *can* choose in America. In most countries you do not get the choice of what you do. Therefore, take advantage of your freedom in America in choosing your career with intentionality and appreciation. The faster you figure out your goals the better.

Many people believe that if you love your job, you haven't worked a day in your life. I'd say that the individual that loves what they do is living their dream. Wouldn't you? Pursue your dreams because you can live big. It's never too late to start.

LAYING THE FOUNDATION FIRST

A lot of success icons will tell you to follow your passions. They usually neglect to tell you that you need to lay a foundation and safeguard yourself financially first. Your initial job may not be your dream job, but you do need to lay that foundation first and get on your feet.

There are many ways to prosper and become wealthy. You do need to love the path that you choose. You don't want to become a millionaire and hate your entire life.

I know of older men in their 60s who can't get a job because their particular field that they chose wasn't working out for them. Unfortunately, they had no backup degrees, training, or different licenses to safeguard themselves. I'll repeat myself: you need to lay the foundation first. Get the degrees or certificates if those are the building blocks to your career—especially if your company will pay for it! Please, don't get me wrong. It is never too late to lay a foundation. I know of another man who, in his mid-50s started an entirely new career path. At 60 years old, he is now promoting and pursuing living bigger.

Most of us accept that we need to do something with our lives. The most frustrating thing is that no one can tell you what you should do—unless you live in a communistic nation of course, but you get the point. All the career assessment tests in the world cannot pinpoint what you should do with your life, but here are some great points to narrow the search.

Where You Live is Where You Work

Choosing your career, or deciding to change careers, will have more to do with where you live than you think.

You have to move your "business" to where there is effective demand. Move to an area where your skill set, or desired skill set is in effective demand—meaning that people can actually afford your product or service.

When I was in Ho Chi Min, Vietnam, I went shopping for suits. While I was picking out fabrics and getting measured, a couple of Americans came in. I naturally started a conversation with them and found out that they were there because they owned their own business and one of their suppliers was in Vietnam. They moved to Vietnam because of their occupation.

The best investment bankers are in New York City. The best computer geniuses are in Silicon Valley. The fashion gurus are in

How to Choose a Career

Los Angeles, NYC, or Paris. I have lived in Los Angeles for four years. My wife was born and raised there, and I have a ton of friends who work in the fashion industry and guess what, they don't live in Kentucky or Ohio.

Know the economic situation in the area before you move to a new location. Example: If the economy in the area is almost entirely based on farming and factory work, then don't move there unless you are a farmer or you want to work in a factory.

If you were born and raised, or are currently living in a small town—and by small I mean less than 200,000 people, like it or not, your economy is based on one or two industries. So, if your skill set matches those jobs that are in demand in your area, you are in luck. If not, you have to move or learn to like the jobs in your area. If this sounds fatalistic to you, keep reading. There is a solution to this.

Supply and Demand

In Los Angeles, the average house price was around $500,000. My next door neighbor in Ohio sold his house for twenty thousand and the city gave him twenty thousand as a stimulus plan to renovate it. Why was there such a difference? Hopefully, this section will help.

Choosing a career and location needs to be very intentional. First, find a demand, and then fill that demand. See how much demand there is for your skill set, and look at the top incomes for that area. If the richest people in your field are not making your desired income, then you know that you probably won't either. Go ahead and cross that location off of your list. You know at that point that there is not enough demand to allow you to bring in your desired income.

Dream Big Live Bigger

If the top household incomes are making as much as you would like to make, move on to step 2 (a); surveying the competition. See how many people in your field are making that amount. If only the top 10% of Computer Programmers are making $70,000 in that area, then you know that you would need to make it into the top 10% to make that amount. Depending on your skill level, confidence, experience, and sometimes, who you know, you may want to move to this location and fight to make it into the top 10%.

Next, see if the location is saturated. Consider this step 2 (b). Accountants should see how many accountants there are; lawyers see how many lawyers there are. If there are too many professionals in your field, it will be particularly difficult to compete. If the community has a pizza place on every corner, regardless of your skill level, it will be much harder to break into the top 10%. It is always easier to make your desired income if you are a big fish in a small pond.

States Compete for You

All fifty states in the United States are competing for your residency. If you watch television, then you have seen the commercials that command you to move to this state or that state. This is because when more productive citizens move to their state, the healthier the economy is in that state; and the state gets your tax money. Therefore, every state will have incentives for people to move there. Maybe there is no state income tax, maybe they give large corporations tax breaks so that they will move factories into their smaller towns. Pay attention to each state's incentives and factor these in when you are making the decision of where to live.

The vast majority of Americans, in contrast, typically pick their location based on family or weather. Shouldn't we move to a place that's the most tax favorable, and have the lowest cost of living? Shouldn't we get on our feet before we can have the luxury of making decisions based on preferences?

After moving from Los Angeles to Houston our cost of living dropped 42%. Texas has no income tax, and the price of housing is a fraction of the cost.

Moving to another state is not necessarily the best decision at all times, but these are principles to consider.

Starting Out Small

Most businesses start out in a garage or small area in a house. Why don't we start out life in a small apartment, or even share a room? Most Americans take out a mortgage for a large amount of money to buy a house. This normally turns out to be a hindrance because you limit your future options while not being fully on your feet. Plus these people normally can't afford any of the necessary repairs or the property taxes on their large home. When you learn how to manage a smaller home, you are that much more equipped to move into a bigger home when the time is opportune. Don't get in over your head in responsibility, especially when starting out in life.

Limiting Your Options

Everyone should strive to keep as many doors open as possible. When you have less money because you collect objects, like house décor, you have fewer resources to invest.

No, I don't necessarily mean only investing in stocks or mutual funds. Investing could be formal education or buying storage units to rent out, but it also could include helping a friend move across country (investing in other people). All the options you could have had are quickly eradicated when you spend your resources on things and activities that are, at best, worthless. I understand that certain activities and objects might bring you comfort, but if you find your comfort in inanimate objects or wasteful activities—especially those expenditures that harm you—then at best you are simply choosing to limit your options.

When I was younger I applied to become an officer in the United States Air Force. At the time, it was extremely competitive and they had a very strict vetting process. First off, you had to fill out packets of paperwork. In these documents were questions about your character like: Have you ever consumed any illegal substances? Have you had any children out of wedlock? Have you ever gotten a speeding ticket? Or, do you have any tattoos? When we went over this packet during the first meeting the recruiter said, "If you've answered yes to any of these questions, you might as well get up out of your seats and leave now." I remember it like it was yesterday.

How to Choose a Career

At first, I thought that it was very interesting that those were their standards. Then I thought to myself, "Where did they get those standards?" But regardless, if I answered yes to any of those questions I was not welcomed to move on to the next step, and I would have just limited my options. I am not saying that you are an unforgivable sinner if you answered yes to any of these questions. I'm just making a point. You never know what the future holds, so keep your options as open as possible.

Going Virtual

If your dream is being financially independent, then this section is for you.

Start an online business. There is no faster and better way to make passive income and become financially free. When you have an online source of income, it doesn't matter where you live, the same exact principles of supply and demand apply. There are no excuses to not be rich, especially with the internet and social media.

Have a service that you can provide from anywhere in the world, like getting a C.P.A. license. You can live anywhere in the world and still produce financial statements, prepare tax returns, or do some consulting work. This is made even easier with video conferences.

CREATE YOUR OWN PRODUCT

Creating your own product is the culmination of this entire chapter. You don't want to choose a job, and then be enslaved to that job until you are forced to retire.

Dream Big Live Bigger

Have a service or product that you can sell using the internet. Free yourself up to live out your dreams and fulfill your potential. When you do have the freedom to do whatever you want with your day, your genius will be freed. Your mind will have the time to research; you won't be as distracted or oppressed so you can finally spread your wings.

Do What You Want to Do

You have to want success. I was once asked why I know so much about accounting and writing off expenses. The fact is that I just hate paying taxes so much that I learned about it. There is emotion and passion involved. I hate paying taxes so much that I'm willing to do something about it.

Now that you've thought through some extremely practical and helpful steps, it's time to ask yourself one question: what do you want to do? It may sound simple, but as long as you're not doing something destructive or illegal begin pursuing whatever you want to.

Everyone does what they want to do, at all times. So now simply take that natural principle, apply the tips in this chapter, and move forward. Let me lay heavy emphasis on moving forward. Pursue what you want. You have to get going.

COUNT THE COST

My mother always told me to make a 'Pros and Cons' list. It's normally easy to come up with the 'Pros' list, all the benefits of a choice, but I urge you to weigh the 'Cons' more heavily. Joining the military has a lot of benefits, but the 'Cons' might out-weigh the 'Pros,' even though there are numerically more 'Pros.' Focus on qualitative aspects, not quantitative.

13. GIVE YOURSELF A RAISE

If you have ever played Monopoly, you know that competing to win is much easier when you have more money than your competitors. In pursuing your full potential, one of the goals has to be obtaining money. The problem is that you can't count on a raise at work, and even if you do, it will usually be an infinitesimal amount. Now I'm going to tell you the secrets of giving yourself a raise.

When Your Boss Has No Choice

My supervisor asked me to come in to work on Saturday so that the shop workers could finish their project. If our customer didn't get the materials from us on Saturday, we would lose our customer's account, which was worth hundreds of thousands of dollars a year.

I wasn't able to be there, so the plant manager had to come in at 7:45 p.m. on a Saturday. They stayed until 3 a.m. in order to finish the job.

Now how in the world does a boss not give the two workers a raise, or, at least, a bonus for giving up their Saturday nights with their families? You can never be guaranteed that your boss will give you a raise at work, but you can definitely raise your chances. Here's how:

Don't be afraid to work more than eight hours a day, five days a week, especially until your financial snowball has gained momentum. We are still laying the foundation at this point by beefing up the savings. Don't worry. Working long hours should not continue for long.

133

Work on the weekends. If your boss doesn't want to give you overtime, offer to work at your regular rate. I began working from home on the weekends, and I saved my boss from hiring a second office employee. I also greatly benefitted because the checks were much bigger from the extra hours. Always do more than you are expected to do. Make your boss love the fact that you work there.

Work to better your skills when you are off the clock. Study and research ways to improve your efficiency at work while you are at home. This lesson is absolutely essential when you are early in your career. However, it is still a mentality to have a decade down the road too.

Have a side job if you need to gather more savings. We are just preparing for freedom. If you are stuck living paycheck to paycheck because your wages are too low, consider a side job. Again, we are being radical. Time is ticking.

14. THE TRUTH BEHIND BUDGETING

You need to know exactly how much income you have and what your expenses are. That is exactly what a budget helps you with.

In my experience, people don't want a budget because they are lazy and are passively choosing to struggle financially throughout life, or they don't want to give up things that they know they actually can't afford. The ultimate reason for not having a budget is that they just don't want to be successful enough. They simply don't care enough. You have to care enough to do something about it.

If you can't seem to get ahead financially, hopefully, this section will help.

Cut Your Expenses

Cutting your expenses begins with keeping a record of your expenses. I know that seems obvious, but on the off-hand that you actually don't keep a ledger or a budget, I'm telling you now that you need to. At least, you need to in order for you to cut your expenses to the best of your ability.

When I was a child my grandpa Charlie showed me his ledger. He kept track of every penny that came in and out of his possession; this ledger was hand-written. Most people don't even use computer software to keep a budget. How much more determination do you think it took to hand write everything?

Cut down on your grocery bill by spending less. Buy drinks that are less expensive. Buy water instead of your normal purchase of juice or soda. Neither sugary option is good for you anyway.

Dream Big Live Bigger

Whenever you buy something ask yourself if you can get it cheaper or can get it for free. You would be surprised how much you can get for free.

One of the best areas to cut down expenses in is entertainment. Don't go to a movie theater to watch movies. You know you can see that movie cheaper by getting it on the internet, and you get to watch it from the comfort of your home. You also save yourself up to $15. What could you do with that extra $15? I know I can do a lot of things.

The second best category to cut down in is your food budget. Save yourself time and money by not eating out. Shop at a grocery store that serves your needs, yet doesn't overcharge for groceries.

Next, get rid of your "personal fun money" category. You may have heard of people putting a "personal" category where that person has allotted themselves a certain amount of money to buy whatever they want without feeling guilty. Instead, create a budget with only categories that are absolutely necessary. Then see how low each category can go.

You would be surprised by how little you can live off of. The first year I lived in Los Angeles I lived off of $14,000. You would also be amazed at how much you can cut in each category. My wife changed which store she bought groceries from and cut our food category in half—literally half.

But this also requires a lot of "sacrifice." I put quotations because I am referring to expenses that simply shouldn't exist. I'm not saying you can never buy ice cream. The point is to lay the foundation, give yourself some options, and get the financial snowball rolling down the hill.

How Much Should You Save?

I'm sure you have heard different ways to save. Most likely you have heard it stated in terms of percentages, like save 10% or 15%. Or perhaps you have heard people say it in terms of different portions, ratios, fractions, etc. All of them are wrong. You need to save every single penny you can. Forget about the percentages; forget about the fractions. Keep your expenses as low as humanly possible.

Living Way Below Your Means

Some are not living below their means because their cost of living is so high. Therefore, they must make a certain amount of money to make ends meet. In other words, their income needs to meet their expenses.

You need to be as flexible as possible. In order to do that, you have to live below your means by a lot. Almost everyone I know who lives in Los Angeles is living above their means and they are in a deep hole of debt. They might be living it up, but their net worth is negative.

When you are living above your means it is also much harder to get a new job. If you get laid off, you must take a job that pays about the same. A lot of people would like to quit their jobs and take another, but they can't. They have no choice. If you were already living above your means, and barely making your payments on your debt, how can you afford to make less? You need to live below your means to stay flexible.

Now, if your expenses are way below your income, you have all the flexibility in the world. You can save tons of money, and get on the career track you want. You can go back to school, or do whatever you want.

WASTING MONEY

There is a principal in the computer world called GIGO (garbage in, garbage out). It states that if you put faulty data into a computer, the resulting information will also be faulty. The same is true in life. If you do a bad job handling your money, you will always have bad results.

Don't be Mastered by Anything

Don't be mastered by stuff. Don't collect things unless that is your big dream. Even then you better have everything else paid for first, like a fully funded retirement plan and your kids' college. Pretty much no one should collect anything unless you are trading it to make a profit. But most people aren't collecting to invest, so this probably doesn't apply to most.

I won't get into the psychology of why people "collect" because every case is different. Just understand that collecting for collecting sake is normally not a good thing. Financially speaking, it is a huge drain on the bank account. If you can, start selling your stuff that you don't need.

EXCISE TAX

Wasting money on cigarettes and alcohol will slow the progress of reaching your goals. Have you ever heard of Excise tax, or "Sin Tax?" Even the government knows that these products are harmful to society, so they place a very high tax on them.

A research project in 2011 revealed that the average smoker spends between $1,500 to $3,300 on cigarettes a year. Time Magazine says that smoking can cost you between one million and two million in a lifetime.

The Truth Behind Budgeting

Regardless if smoking and drinking are a sin, they're financially irrational purchases. Also, drinking dehydrates brain cells, thereby killing them. If you want to reach your full potential, you're going to need all the brain cells you can get.

Products with excise tax are designed to enslave you and waste your money.

DON'T BUY SPORTS CARS

When I lived in Hollywood, I drove a Camaro with an engine bigger than most pickup trucks and a sporty, Mercedes convertible, but it turns out that the speed limit is the same for everyone. The Camaro had just less than 300 horsepower, but I could only use about 100 of them. What's the point? The insurance was more expensive, the gas was more expensive, and the maintenance was more expensive. The cost out-weighed the benefits.

Unless you are legally getting paid to race, don't buy a sports car.

The Value of $10

Sam Walton knew the value of money. When he was getting his picture taken, a buddy put a dime on the ground near him. At the time, Sam was already rich, but the friend wanted to test him to see what he would do. He walked over to the dime and asked the photographer if he was supposed to stand right over this dime to get his picture taken.

If you ask most Americans if $10 was a lot of money, they would probably say no. If you asked a millionaire, they would probably say yes. We all need to appreciate every dollar more.

Let me tell you how powerful ten dollars is. It is the difference between having lunch and going hungry. It is gas money to drive to work and back. It is survival for a day and if rationed, maybe even a few. When you live at low means, you can get more out of every dollar.

When you begin to think about what you could do with $10, you will be less likely to waste it. This point will not directly give you a raise, but it will indirectly. You will be more intentional with your money.

Going Above And Beyond

A GOOD JOB IS NOT ENOUGH

Most of us will have bosses; at least for a season. This principle can help you get a raise, or at least, keep you from being fired. I can go through the motions and get tasks done perfectly, but if I'm not making my boss happy, I'm not doing a good job overall. Pleasing your boss is 'value added,' and adding value normally means adding money.

Always do more work than you're expected to do. I don't mean that you should be directly disobedient and do something in which you have no training for and destroy a machine worth tens of thousands of dollars. Do more beneficial tasks. You need to make sure that the benefit of keeping you there is more than the cost of your employment. Always do more than you are paid for.

Let others know that you can do different tasks that need to be done, and volunteer to do them. Only do this if you actually can do the task, of course. The more value you bring, the more you will get paid.

The Truth Behind Budgeting

One of the persons you need to have the best customer service with is your boss. As an employee, you are hired to have impeccable customer service. Since you are hired, your boss is purchasing your value. Your boss is technically now a customer in the sense of their purchase. Give your boss the best customer service that you can give. If you don't prefer the term customer service, then give your boss the best *boss service* that you can give. Regardless, you are hired as a service provider. Serve with sacrifice. A lot of days are ahead of you that you will need to forego your "right" to be right.

GIVE YOUR BOSS A RECEIPT

This principle works especially when your boss is mad at you. Make a breakdown of your daily tasks and how long it took you to complete each task, a.k.a. a daily log.

Giving your boss a receipt will calm him or her down because you are reminding your boss of the benefits of your employment. They can look at the "receipt" and see *what* you were able to do, and *how quickly* you were able to do them.

ALWAYS BE PREPARED TO GIVE AN ANSWER

Always be prepared to answer questions about your job or a task. While you're doing the task, ask the people around you questions and gather up all the answers. If you can't remember the details, write them down.

You already know that your supervisor needs information from you in order to make their decisions, and the quicker you are at giving them the information, and the more accurate you are, the better.

NEVER MAKE THE SAME MISTAKE TWICE...LITERALLY

Mistakes happen. Don't dwell on whose fault it is. Instead, try to learn from the situation. Every time a mistake happens— regardless of whose fault it is—setup at least one brand new system that will make it extremely difficult to make the same mistake twice.

Being a part of startup companies gave me the opportunity to apply this principle first hand. We customized and built dump trucks and sold them all over the nation. Every single piece of paperwork crossed my desk. After a sale was made there were thirty-five different steps that needed to be handled; from warranties, financing, titles, registration, and to most everything else.

At first, I tried to use post-it notes to keep up. As you already know, that wasn't going to work. At any given point I needed to keep track of about thirteen different truck transactions. Each truck was either in the beginning, middle, or end of the sale process; and remember, there were thirty-five stages that needed to be completed for each one.

After failing a few times to keep up, I started using a software program to help keep everything perfectly organized. From then on I instantly had the answers to every question.

Analyze every problem or issue before making your evaluation of it. Do your best to learn from the situation. Then you can, at least, think of a solution. Consider the problem and come up with a direct way to stop it from ever happening again, regardless of who's at fault.

Attitude

Don't let your attitude or actions be the reason you don't get a raise. Don't let *'you'* be the reason you don't get a raise.

Keeping your attitude free from anger, bitterness, resentment, envy, and pride will always be necessary. Don't make the mistake of nurturing any of these bad attitudes. Consider adding, "check my heart attitude" to your to-do list each day. No matter the attacks thrown at you through the day, it will be the correct heart attitude that will prevail.

People don't like to do business with, nor have, employees who possess a bad attitude. Those are typically the first contacts to go, even despite the value of their business. Likewise, an employee will be fired more quickly for a poor attitude, no matter how talented a worker they are. Remember that you may not be the MVP of your company. Let that be a warning not to think there isn't competition stepping in from behind you.

15. THE TRUTH BEHIND LEADERSHIP

At one time or another you have been, are now, or will be a leader.

Leadership is a high calling, but what exactly is a leader? A leader is someone who goes before a group of people and shows them the way by different means. Leaders guide, direct, and even command. Each of these aspects of leadership is weighty. The person making commands must have solid reasoning behind them. A leader is in a position of authority that holds others in their care.

There Can Only Be One

In every group setting there absolutely must be, and will be, one leader. This is one reason why everyone scans a room when entering a situation. They naturally want to find their role in the pecking order.

There can only be one Alpha. Why would we care if someone is smarter, faster, or better in any way? We are determining who the alpha is.

If you don't have a leader in a group setting then nothing will get done. Someone has to have initiative, have information, and so on.

Never exalt yourself to this position of leadership. As you are reading this book, I am sure that you are relating with many points. You may feel at this section that you are someone who desires to be a leader. The fact that you began reading this book points out that you have a desire to know more than the average person.

Typically knowledge seekers are also authority seekers. We want to use our knowledge to guide others. It is a completely natural correlation. However, do not demand that you are a leader and do not go forth assuming that you are. Every season will prove differently in who has the role of teaching or instructing. In some seasons, you may only be a learner.

Also, I will warn you not to be surprised when others will not listen to your advisement. There are many people who do not want knowledge and are envious that you do want it. I know it seems absolutely irrational because it really is lacking logic. A large majority of people do not want to change nor do they want to be lead. Your wealth of knowledge may repel certain individuals like water and oil. Don't be discouraged. It is about finding the binding agent that can merge the oil with the water that will have people following you. Binding agents are humility and love. Practice guiding those who want to be helped with the perspective that you are no better than they are.

RISING LIKE CREAM

Leaders rise to the top like cream. It happens pretty naturally. There are certain attributes that greatly contribute to your ability to rise to the top, and these qualities will be discussed in the rest of this chapter.

There are particular times where the one with the best leadership qualities is not the leader, but these are the exceptions. This default, or presumed leader, can stay at the top only if he or she fulfills their role. For example, the head of the household is assumed to be the leader, but the head of the house will quickly lose the leadership role if a stronger leader enters the group—unless the stronger leader actively submits to the weaker leader.

Having followers doesn't make you a good or a knowledgeable leader, it can also mean that your followers are more mature and follow out of a love and desire to be at peace.

Every time a group is formed, the leader is picked. It is the very first thing that happens. We look for strengths, but we also look for weaknesses. Inferior qualities can be as simple as having a bad haircut, or having a "bad" hair style. Our minds conclude that they are not as proactive to get up in the morning to get themselves ready, or that they have bad judgment, or they are just uglier than us.

As trite as this sounds, it is true. It is the reason bullies pick on students "inferior" to them. They are reasserting their "alpha-ness." More on this later.

DON'T USURP LEADERSHIP

Be careful not to usurp leadership. For example, if you are a guest at someone's party. Defer to others. If there is an established leader already, let them lead.

Pay close attention to the host's reactions. If you are speaking too openly, they may show intimidation and react. Gage yourself and shy away from coming off too strong at their home.

The power is really in the follower's hands. When two or more people vote you out of leadership, assume the position of now being a follower. You no longer have the role that you thought you had and have been vetoed. Usurping authority at this time will only make your fall that much worse.

TOO MANY MISTAKES

As a leader, you are not allotted too many mistakes before your followers begin to lose their confidence in you. Mistakes may show that you are not yet ready to guide others. Your team needs to be confident in your decision-making skills.

So what are some of the characteristics of a good leader? A qualified leader is first and foremost, trusted.

Your followers need to trust in your creativity, your decision-making process, your execution of the plan, and trust that you will succeed.

TRUST

Trust is the key component of all relationships. It is no wonder that the same would be required between leaders and followers.

People trust those who:

1. Have their follower's best interest in mind.

2. Have the ability to carry it out.

Having other people's well-being in mind is foundational to building trust with them. Employees will not trust a boss who short cuts them or makes decisions at their expense. A wise boss will care for their employees knowing that the employee has a family that they have to care for. If you neglect employees, they,

148

in turn, will take the real heat when they can't provide best for their loved ones.

You also have to build trusting partnerships. A business partner putting themselves on the line is taking a risk assuming that you will not give them the short end of the stick.

In fact, the clearest way to communicate care for your employees, partners, or anyone is to take the short end of the stick and give them the long end. Of course, this can't be ridiculous, but I am talking sacrifices. When others realize the sacrifices you make for them, then they can rest assured knowing that you wouldn't harm the ones you sacrifice yourself for.

Trust does not stand on sacrifice alone, though. Having the ability to carry out plans and promises is the second component of building trust. Following through with commitments and plans conveys that you won't fall short. These are qualities that can be trusted. If you prove to me that you are looking out for my best interest and can follow through, you will have my allegiance.

HAVING ANSWERS

Have you ever heard someone tell you that, "leaders read, and readers lead?" Well, reading is the difference between the haves and the have-nots.

Knowing more about something is the trump card in leadership. Knowledge really is power, especially in this case. This principle is true in any circumstance. If you have more knowledge than others in a group, age doesn't matter.

The only exception is if someone has a lot more money than you, and is financing a deal. In this case, the one with the most knowledge might not be making the final decision, but most of the time they will be influencing the one with the money to such a degree that they might as well be.

A salesman will convince someone with money to buy something.

My sales manager convinced people to buy a dump truck worth $120,000. He did this because he knew more about dump trucks than any human being who ever lived. Most of the sales calls were an educational seminar. Because of this, people would wire us on average $100,000, sight unseen.

If you have more knowledge than the next person, you will be in leadership because they will ask you for advice. Being a leader means having answers. If anything needs to be done, the leader is ultimately responsible. This is easier said than done.
A leader says, "The problem was this, and here's how I fixed it."

A leader also has good judgment and takes in all the information. They make calculated risks by considering the pros and cons. They factor in what could not only be lost by themselves, but more importantly, what others could lose.

LEADERS ARE VISIONARIES

Leaders are visionaries. If they don't have a vision and if they don't have a plan, they will desperately think and research until they have one.

Delegating

Delegating isn't difficult once you know the principles. You have to find the right person in the right place for the right job. Here is another principle to consider…there are no "bad" jobs. There will be someone, somewhere, who wants to do any given job.

I hate grocery shopping. I hate shopping period. I always say that I would rather dig a hole to China. My wife doesn't mind grocery shopping, so she does the shopping. Some people get a sense of accomplishment from entering data into a spreadsheet. Some people like to clean. There aren't any inherently "bad" jobs, just bad delegation. There are jobs that most don't enjoy, but machines are starting to do those jobs anyway. Leaders know how to match the right person to the right job.

LEADERS WORK ALONGSIDE OTHERS

A leader always delegates smaller tasks to others, but always takes on the bigger ones themselves. If you don't work alongside and help out, people will resent it. They won't feel appreciated, and instead, they feel more like slaves.

When you are delegating, tell them why you are having them do the tasks, double check their work, but…

Be especially sensitive to their personalities.

Know who you are talking to. You don't want to provoke anyone to anger. You will never get the most out of others working abilities if they are upset. The measure of productivity is directly correlated to their happiness and contentment.

16. THE TRUTH BEHIND MOTIVATION

What is Motivation?

Motivation is the driving force behind success. It is why we do what we do. To break this down further, we must go deeper into motivation.

Again, people do what they want to do. They have to do what they want to do; they have no choice. They are slaves to their desires. We will always do what we believe is in our best interest at any given moment. We do what we want to do most in any particular situation.

WHAT IS SELF-MOTIVATION?

Why are you reading this book?

WHAT MOTIVATES YOU?

Two components of motivation exist: past achievements and belief in capabilities of future achievements. When you get weighed or bogged down by the hindrances that are in the way of your success, you forget these two motivators. You doubt that they are true of you. This is where an outside source of encouragement comes into play. We all need someone else to remind us that we are capable.

Some people are not self-motivated. They are too insecure to believe that they are capable of great things. These are the people that rely SOLELY on others to continually feed them encouragement. This encouragement becomes their only source of energy, and after a while most encouragers find this a daunting task to be someone's personal motivator. It may even label (blacklist) this person as a bad investment because, despite their potential, their insecurities are far too great to overcome. Until you get over your insecurities, you will always be your greatest de-motivator.

Are you this person that needs a fan club in order to be successful?

17. HOW TO TRULY INFLUENCE PEOPLE

Now that we understand motivation, we have to ask the question, how do we influence others to do what we want them to do? This principle is essential for getting ahead in life and living out your dreams.

The answer is very simple. Make them believe that what you want them to do is better for them than what they would have done otherwise. The goal is to tip the scale of their desires. Most of the time influence is made without literally saying these words.

DIRECT INFLUENCE

I once saw a display of direct influence shown by a speaker to his audience. The speaker began by calling a volunteer onto the stage. The volunteer was told to sit in a chair in the middle of the stage; the presenter was about to illustrate how motivation works.

Bets were made between the speaker and the volunteer of how long he would stay in the chair without getting up. The volunteer wanted to stay in the chair for a certain amount of time in order to win his bet, but there was no real prize for winning. Within a couple of seconds, the speaker showed the volunteer cold hard cash; the volunteer got up right away, took the money, and left the stage. The speaker won.

People will do a lot...almost anything—including looking dumb—for the right dollar amount.

The incentive of money tilted the scales of what the volunteer wanted to do. Once the speaker made the volunteer believe that it was in his best interest to get up out of the seat, and lose the bet, it was over.

This is a perfect, yet simple example of how every human being thinks. People will do things when asked, only if it benefits them. Sometimes the only benefit for them is having their ego stroked. It reinforces the thought that they are a "good" person. They will help out others for the incentive of self-affirmation or praise from others.

With that being said; when telling someone what to do, try forming it into a question. It takes all of the edges off and doesn't offend people. Commanding people to do things makes them not want to do it. Here are some examples:

Could you email this document for me?

Are you going to be able to come in on Saturday?

INDIRECT INFLUENCE

Influencing others directly with bribery is much different than influencing others indirectly. If you have ever had someone look up to you, you know what I'm talking about.

I can change how frequent people shower, what they eat, how much they exercise, etc., etc. I know that as long as someone looks up to me and wants to be like me, they will believe that it is in their best interest to listen to my advice.

Having wisdom allowed me to give parenting advice to an ER doctor on a plane. He even offered to let me stay at his house too.

How to Truly Influence People

I was flying from Los Angeles to Houston and I happened to be sitting next to an ER doctor. He was telling me about his trip to Israel and we just kept talking. Because I was able to converse with him intelligently, I was able to build credibility. He began to trust that I knew what I was talking about, and before long he was asking me for parenting advice—even though I had *never* been a parent. I was about twenty-seven years old and he was pushing sixty.

To live out your dreams, you need to understand how influence works because every human interaction hinges on this principle. Bullies at school pick on smaller, less popular kids because the benefits outweigh the consequences. Children disobey their parents because the benefits outweigh the consequences.

The Golden Rule

A self-centered man is a discontented man.

What if we treated other people the way we wanted to be treated? Instead, what people normally do is treat the people closest to them the worst. There are countless stories of people taking on a partnership with their close friends or family and treating one another worse than anyone else. I know of a mother and daughter partnership where this was the case. There was less patience displayed toward the daughter, with the mother seeming to take everything out on her. She actually treated the employees better than her own family.

This shouldn't be the case. Do not allow yourself to treat people with partiality or, in this case, extreme impartiality with those who are closest. Keep to the golden rule.

GIVE CREDIT WHERE CREDIT IS DUE

Misleading or taking the credit for a job well done is both thievery and lying. Don't be a liar and a thief; give credit to the correct source.

If you want to win friends, employees, or contacts of any sort, praise their work whenever the time calls for it.

Volunteering is Networking

Whenever you decide to volunteer, you place yourself in the perfect position to not only come to the aid of others who require assistance, but also get to know many other people. Some of these people may become your biggest fans. Allow yourself the opportunity of getting to know others in an ideal setting such as serving. When you serve alongside someone, you build a bond. It may not be a close bond, but it is one that you now have that you didn't have before, and wouldn't have had if you merely went out of your way to pass out your business card. Volunteering is a huge way to let yourself be known. You promote who you are, what you stand for, and potentially what you are good at.

If you are able to, it's better for you to volunteer in something that you are gifted in. In doing this you open the doors to not only serving to a larger degree, but to more effective networking as well. Now, before you think that networking is using this situation, keep in mind that there is nothing wrong with networking. I'm not saying to volunteer for the *sole purpose* of self-advertisement, or that you should go hard in self-promotion. What I am saying is that networking is getting to know many people. They can be a great resource to you later, and you can be a great resource for them as well.

How to Truly Influence People

In the many volunteer programs that I have been privileged to be a part of, I have gotten to know an abundance of different kinds of awesome individuals. These people have contacted me later, asking me for advice. Likewise, I have contacted several friends from past volunteer events to ask them for their help in future events.

You see, networking is about making friends. Volunteering automatically puts you in the realm of others who like to give and serve like you. The more you have in common, the better your friendships may flourish. Sometimes if you put yourself in places to make friendships, you put yourself in the means of making business advancements. It's not about using people it's about networking. The larger the network, the more traffic you will get.

As a Cosmetologist, my wife once volunteered to cut hair at a local church event. She had heard about the event through a friend who had asked her to help there. My wife went and joyfully served alongside complete strangers. After the event ended, she had countless people asking for her information so that they could go to her for their cosmetology needs. Some of these people included ones with whom she had served alongside, while others were strangers that had stood nearby overhearing her speaking to the children and their parents as she cut their hair.

My wife left that day with many fans, although that was not her intention. When asked by the pastor of the church if there was any way that they could return the favor, she told them that caring for others *was* serving her.

Networking is about making connections. Marketing is about making fans. Sometimes the two overlap and you have great connections who are fans.

Being at Peace with All Men

The following quick points will take you very far in life.

THE POWER OF 'HMMMMMS' AND 'HUHS'

I often use phrases like 'hmmm,' 'huh,' and 'I hear ya.' One of my personal favorites is, "That's one way of looking at it."

It takes a lot of trial and error to master this skill, but this is a way to disagree completely with someone without offending them. Find a way *not* to disagree with others as much as possible.

STOPPING GOSSIP

For some reason, people love to talk about others behind their backs. I understand why they do it. They want to put others down so that they can be elevated. This too is illogical in the truest sense because the accuser is only putting themselves down. But because gossip is a reality, we need to learn how to handle it. It's simple. Whenever someone starts to gossip, say, "I don't have all the information, so I can't comment." Or maybe even defend the person being talked about.

Never talk bad about anyone at any time, no exceptions.

"Venting" is gossip's big sister, and it never helps a situation either. I suppose everyone vents. Venting is us trying to justify ourselves by putting others down. It is the result of pride being offended because we are too immature to handle not getting our way. We think venting helps us 'get it off our chest,' but it only embitters us, and we end up dwelling on it. In most cases we dwell on imperfect and incomplete facts. Ergo, venting is illogical. Yet, we all still do it every day. (More on this later)

Instead, write down the facts that you know are true, and if you need to, write down what you feel. That way you can look back over time and see how much you have matured over the years. It's a great source of encouragement. Of course, make sure no one ever reads it.

P.S.--Be very careful when putting something in writing. You can never take it back. The best you can do is seek forgiveness, and there is never a guarantee that the person who read what you wrote will forgive you.

OTHER OFFENSIVE SPEECH

Phrases that should probably never come out of your mouth:
"Who are you?"
"Of course…"
"What are you talking about?"
"Don't do that!"
"What are you doing?!"

Don't start a sentence with the interrogative 'Why.' This is almost always offensive. You can easily change a sentence starting with why to, "Oh, what's that for?

SILENCE IS GOLDEN

The power of silence is powerful, especially as a response to an angry person. The only exception to this is if they ask you a direct question, and you know that they would be provoked if you didn't answer them.

LAUGH AT YOUR OWN MISTAKES

(Pride gets in the way of doing this sometimes.)

I had taken my Camaro to the mechanics for a repair that was meant to solve a stalling/start-up problem. After being called about the repairs being finished, my wife and I went to go pick it up. On my drive home, I began to notice the car was having issues. It was running in and out of power. I pulled over into the first plaza and the car fully lost power. Aggravated with it not working after I had just left the mechanics, I called them back. They were just closing so I had a tow truck come to get my car.

At the arrival of the tow truck service, the guy came over and checked out my Camaro before loading it up onto the truck. He began to laugh and told me, "Man, your tank is on empty." I can't tell you how hard I laughed at myself that day. I was so frustrated with my car problems that I seemed to overlook checking my gas gage. We all make ridiculous actions and have poor responses. Laughter helps you to accept and move past your mistakes.

DON'T PRESS YOUR POINT

Don't press your point, especially when you're going to cause frustration to you and the other person. Is your point worth more than severing a friendship? Hopefully, as you read this you respond with a no. However, I, like you, know how easy it is to really want to press a point. Maybe it's about principle and getting your thought out, but this, mixed with the wrong personality, can be a catastrophe. If you are with someone who wants desperately to be the alpha and continues to cut you off, don't stress getting your thought out. Chances are they won't hear it anyway.

If you are the one who desires to be the dominant one, don't try to press your point until the other person agrees with you. This is a recipe for frustration or in other words provoking others to anger. Agreeance does not equate to who is wrong or right. Many people jump aboard sinking ships. This does not mean that they were making a good judgment call. Nor does this mean that if someone has the majority of agreements that they are correct. You may be correct, but if it's not a hill to die on, don't kill others over it.

Do it After Lunch

If you need to give someone bad news, e.g. fire an employee or give a customer bad news about how you failed to live up to your promises, do it after lunch. People are very irritable before lunch. They become 'Hangry.' They get angry because they are hungry.

18. FITTING IN

John D. Rockefeller said, "The ability to deal with people is as purchasable a commodity as sugar or coffee."[19] "And I will pay more for that ability than for any other under the sun."[20]

In 1 Corinthians 9:20 Paul wrote, "To the Jews he became a Jew, that he might reach the Jews" "to the Greeks he became a Greek that he might win some." Paul, who wrote 13 out of the 27 New Testament books and planted churches during his missionary journeys, knew the importance of fitting in. If you want to be successful, and to live to your fullest potential, do your best to fit in. How we dress, how we speak, and how we act directly affects our ability to be influential.

Popularity Matters

Does popularity matter? I've heard *yes*, and I've heard *no*. Well, let me ask you a couple of questions. Who is the most powerful person in the world? Don't bother looking it up; I'll just tell you; the President of the United States of America. Next question: How does the President of the United States get elected? That's right; a nationwide popularity contest. I understand that the popular vote doesn't necessarily make someone the President because of the Electoral College, but you get my point. Popularity *does* matter. Your reputation *does* matter. It matters every phase of life to one degree or another, and it matters in every profession.

If people like you, they will help you. They will give you their money, time, knowledge, and wisdom. Make as many buddies as possible. Why wouldn't you?

Don't Show Partiality

To reach your fullest potential treat everyone the same. This will speak more about your class and the caliber of person you are than you think.

People are always watching, so always be on your 'A' game with this. And remember that we treat those closest to us the worst—familiarity breeds contempt, so make sure that you're treating everyone the same especially at family gatherings.

It takes my grandma twenty minutes to buy a loaf of bread at the grocery store, and not because of long lines. She usually knows everyone at the store, and everyone wants to talk with her. There are a lot of reasons for this, but one of the reasons is that she treats everyone the same. She treats everyone like they are the President of the United States.

> "The desire for a feeling of importance is one of the chief distinguishing differences between mankind and the animals...
> It is this desire that lures many boys and girls into joining gangs and engaging in criminal activities. This desire makes you want to wear the latest styles, drive the latest cars, and talk about your brilliant children...George Washington wanted to be called "His Mightiness, the President of the United States" and Columbus pleaded for the title "Admiral of the Ocean and Viceroy of India."[21] — Dale Carnegie

Everyone wants to be treated like royalty, so treat everyone like royalty.

Fitting In

I saw this principle again when I met an Ohio congressman at a small fundraiser. I was a young man and was working as a server. The congressman treated me the same as those who paid good money to be there. He introduced himself to me, and we had a small conversation.

Treat everyone like they are important and unique. Treat everyone equal, regardless of their socio-economic class, ethnicity, gender, or especially age (age seems to be one of the biggest hang-ups).

You never know who you are talking to. They could be your next boss. Treat everyone the same.

How to Handle Bullies

Why do bullies pick on other students? Again, they are reasserting their alpha-ness. They are insecure and need to pick on others to feel better about themselves. They need validation for their pride. They want control, but others won't follow.

How do you handle bullies? There is only one way. Break their kneecaps with a bat to show them who is boss!! No, that's horrible, don't do that! The real answer is to kill them with KINDNESS.

In Junior High School there was a group of guys who decided that they didn't like me. I happened to sit next to one of these guys in class. He was older, so he probably failed a grade.

Anyway, one day he asked me for a piece of paper, so I gave him two. The "bully" sitting behind me told him that he wasn't supposed to talk to me. The recipient of my kind gesture said, "Why? He didn't do anything to me." It's difficult for people not to like someone who is nice.

Why We Are Insecure

People are insecure if they believe that you have the power to take something away from them. Rich people are more secure because they don't need or want something from you, and therefore, they are not afraid that you won't give them something or take something away.

Secure people aren't too bothered if you like them or not, and their joy isn't dependent on anyone else. They have nothing to prove, and they aren't living to please anyone.

The problem is that no one is perfectly secure. Maturity and security go hand-in-hand. The more mature you are, the more secure you are.

People Are Watching You

Assume that people are watching you because they probably are. People love to "people watch." The better you look, the more they stare because they want to be like you in some sort of way. People check other people out because they are evaluating who you are and they are comparing you to:

1. Their standard.
2. Themselves.

This is precisely why envy and jealousy sells. This is why star athletes have sponsors. Companies know that people will want to be like star athletes and wear what that star athletes wear, so they sign contracts worth millions of dollars.

Be what others will want to be like—without breaking the other rules in this book. People will begin to look up to you, and they will buy whatever you're selling. This principle applies especially when you're trying to get a job because you are selling yourself. It is in your favor to have others want to be like you. If they don't look up to you, you can't have any influence.

Don't discourage people from looking at you. Don't be annoyed or bothered, but don't seek unnecessary attention either. They will stare, it's a given. Let them; you can't stop it anyway.

It's a good thing that people stare if you're a good example for others to follow.

Knowing is Beautiful

We've all been told not to judge a book by its cover, but we all do it, and we are not going to stop anytime soon. Employers will decide in less than a minute if they want to hire you or not based on appearance. So, like it or not, looks do matter.

Businesses care about appearance: business people have veneers, perfectly groomed hair, and their shoes are shined. We should know the basics of how to match colors and how to tie a tie. Men should know what shirt-stays are and what a lapel is. What kind of lapels are there? Which one do I choose and for what occasion? How do I tie a double Windsor? What is a double Windsor? What color socks should I wear, and why? When should I have facial hair? What are the benefits of facial hair? The list goes on and on and on.

Make sure your clothes fit you. Maybe even have your nice shirts tailored.

Subsection your wardrobe. Have fewer clothes, but better clothes. All your clothes should readily match with your other clothes. You should be able to go into your closet blindfolded and match an outfit.

Businessmen wear a suit and tie. They know that people will take them more seriously and that they will have more credibility by being well-kept. Why do Americans go to Wal-Mart in their pajamas; or go to school in lounging attire?

Also, how people dress conveys respect for the people you are around. It shows respect on both sides. We could offend people if we went to an office party in pajamas. Unless it was a pajama office party, but I'm sure these are rare.

Within the first 30 seconds, people already have a first impression. We don't want our attire to be a distraction or a stumbling block, or convey anything but excellence at all times.

Fewer is Better

Be as succinct in your speech as possible. Avoid rephrasing things, unless you're a pastor, teacher, or have specifically been asked to clarify. Practice getting your point across with fewer words. If you catch yourself repeating your point, stop! Don't finish your sentences if you don't have to. (Did you notice how redundant this paragraph is?)

If you catch someone else being redundant, you can't stop them. People frown upon that. Let them say their piece; it helps them.

Don't Be a Walking Billboard

Chew on this:

Do everything in your power to wear clothes that don't have labels on them.

If you go to any store, you can buy hats, gloves, coats, plates, and blankets with that company's name on it. What is happening is they are making a product and an advertisement at the same time. You pay them so that you can advertise for them. Doesn't that seem backward?

Don't wear hats or clothes with school names, state names, or city names. I'm sure you've seen people wear hats that say their favorite city; statistically speaking *you* probably have one too. Remember colleges, states, and cities are all businesses that are competing in the market place. They should be paying you to advertise for them. This is all more of a training process than direct application. We need to get into a mind frame of how money in the market works.

Don't Be a Distraction

Behave the way that others behave. (You'll be hanging out with successful people who don't do stupid things anymore.) Talk as polite as to not offend others around you.

Don't wear distracting clothing, or have distracting features. We want to fit in. Don't do anything that would be distracting.

Don't chase the attention of others. People love attention. I was running on a treadmill in the gym, and a young man was dancing and playing peek-a-boo with very little clothing. He thought it would be funny to distract me and ruin my workout. Don't be like that guy. Let people focus on what they are doing.

Modesty

Immodest men look immature and insecure. Immodest women look immature and insecure.

Modesty is an age-old subject that is directly tied to the desire for self-exaltation. We all secretly know this, but not all of us realize the ramifications for dressing immodestly. You see, when you dress to attract attention, namely sexual attention, it is coined as immodest.

Men and women that dress for all eyes to be on their physical appearance and to remain there are not fully confident in their intellectual abilities. They seek to make up for their lack of confidence by clinging to the next thing that they think will sell themselves, their appearance.

You won't find older and wiser, mature individuals dressing provocatively. Why? Because they know their worth, and they demand their worth, without even stating it, through their modest attire.

You may be fighting me on this one and thinking I'm being judgmental, but I think we both know the motive behind the way each of us dresses. You may believe that you have the right to wear what you want, but my point is that other people view immodesty as immature. This goes back to my point of shooting yourself in the foot. Forsake your right to wear whatever you want for your right to be successful. I think you will enjoy your odds at scaling to success quicker when you aren't giving outsiders a reason to look down on you.

Fitting In

Friends and Social Skills

THE BAD NEWS

Most of your friends are not really friends. Most of your acquaintances use you for their own pleasure. Think I'm exaggerating? Just move to a different state and see how many of your "friends" call you. Any conversation you have with most people is only to exchange information. There is always some kind of benefit.

> "Andrew Carnegie, the poverty-stricken Scotch lad who started to work at two cents an hour and finally gave away $365 million, learned early in life that the only way to influence people is to talk in terms of what the other person wants."[22]—Dale Carnegie

People don't usually care about you or your interests. They only care about their own interests. They only seem to care about your interest if your interests and their interests intersect. They only care about your interests if it is also in their best interest. This is true and profound. You can argue with it if you want, but to a large measure, it is the unfortunate reality of relationships.

THE GOOD NEWS

It is possible to make people interested in you, but, again, only if they happen to be interested in what you're talking about. For most, this is perfectly obvious; especially if you have ever tried to start a conversation with a total stranger. A stranger doesn't know you, nor do they care about you, but if someone else introduces you and the other person by saying what you both have in common, a conversation can exist. Without someone else introducing you two, it is usually a struggle. You will have to find something in common –something you enjoy or know about— that they enjoy also.

As a teenager, I sold athletic shoes. One day two guys came into the store I worked at. I could tell that they were musicians, so I started a conversation about music. They were there to buy shoes, not to talk about music.

We spoke for a while, and it was brought up that they were drummers, like myself. In a nutshell; they bought a very expensive pair of shoes from me because I sold them on our conversation. I intentionally found common ground to relate on, and the customer enjoyed the conversation. He told me, "I am only buying these shoes because I enjoyed talking with you." Okay, I made him sound more intellectual than he was, he really told me some variation of "because you're cool." After all, we were all young and hip drummers.

And if that's not "cool" enough for you, he also invited me to play music with his band. I went to jam with his band that night. The point is, relate with others, you might not always get invited to join in on a jam session with every customer that walks through your place of work, but it opens up doors.

ARE YOU INTERESTING AND RELATABLE?

Have a story to tell!

Uninteresting people are more prone to make fun of other people. They just don't live interesting lives or do interesting activities, so there isn't anything else to talk about. They normally aren't learning something new and interesting either. So, these people gossip.

Fitting In

Don't be uninteresting. The more interesting you are the more that other interesting people will be attracted to you. You want interesting people to surround you because interesting people usually are the most successful.

Do people think that you are interesting? The best way to check this is to see how many people ask you questions. Questions like these mean that they are interested, "Wow, how long will you be in Singapore for?" Questions that have nothing to do with what you just said, or comments that quickly change the topic mean that they couldn't care any less. When this happens, it usually hurts our pride. You can get resentful, you can accept it, or you can change it. Be someone that others want to relate to; be interesting to others.

It is easy to become offended when others don't ask you questions because we all want to belong and desire to be important. You're obviously not important to the other person if they don't want to get to know you. That can be very offensive, but again, you can't change other people.

GET TO KNOW OTHERS

The only thing you can do is be interested in other people. The problem is that everyone has a difficult time being interested in other people. That includes you and me. But believe me; it is in your best interest to be interested in other people. You need the help of others: to get a job, to help you with home improvements, or to keep you company during the big game.

The helpful thing is that people want others to be interested in them; which works out great because you can pick their brain on topics that interest both parties. All you have to do is ask them to talk about themselves. It sounds manipulative, but it is literally the only way to start a conversation. How are you? How long are you staying? What have you been up to? Tell me about your

175

business? It is not manipulative because it is not done in an unfair manner. It is the only way to converse with another human being.

Don't fake being interested in people because people can see through fake. You have to be genuine. So the trick is to find something that interests both parties. It might be a book sitting on their shelf, a type of car that the other person owns, or what someone's occupation is. Find common ground, and then go from there. Only after you have found common interests can you be animated and enthusiastic. The chain reaction then necessitates that the other person will be interested in you because something about you interests the other person, and you have now gained a buddy, if not a friend.

It is way more beneficial to have someone else talking. You can't learn much if you do all the talking. That said, encourage others to talk about themselves, then be a good listener. Ask others questions that they would enjoy answering.

Mannerisms communicate interest also. There are people who simply light up a room. They attract people to them like a magnet, and they don't repel anyone away. My grandma Sandy is one of those people. Why do people get excited when they meet my grandma? Well, a lot of reasons, but one, in particular, stands out: her smile. She is genuinely excited to see people. It is almost supernatural. I guess her smile literally is supernatural because she has perfectly white veneers, but you get what I mean.

TRIAL AND ERROR

Knowing the basics of interacting with others is great, but we all need to fine-tune our social skills. This takes trial and error. I learned this when I was living on a cruise ship surrounded by the richest, smartest, and most well-traveled human beings who have ever lived. These individuals had their own helicopters and chefs. They also had backgrounds of having attended the most prestigious schools.

Put yourself in situations where you are forced to practice these lessons. You will need to fine tune these skills; they will be important for success.

19. INTEGRITY

This next section is especially important!

ETHICS

Ethics are the understood rules for a particular action and group. To determine if something is ethical, ask yourself if it is illegal; if it negatively affects anyone. Because of its definition, ethics is indisputably the most difficult integrity issue to wrestle through.

I know a missionary from Malawi who asked me if I thought it was ethical for him to buy bootlegged movies in third world countries. That is a very tricky question. What do you think the answer is?

WHAT IS A GOOD DEAL?

A deal is only a good deal if it benefits both parties. It doesn't have to benefit each party equally; it just needs to benefit each party to some measure. Never make a one-sided deal. If the other person senses that you are trying to rip the other person off, they won't want to do the deal, and you won't ever make a deal with them again.

DON'T COMPROMISE ON ABSOLUTES

There are many ways to prosper and become wealthy. Make sure the path that you choose, you love. You don't want to become a millionaire and hate your entire life.

LET YOUR YES BE YES

If you say that you are going to do something, or make someone believe that you are going to do something, do it.

Even if you didn't say "I promise," it's still a promise. Following through with what you say you're going to do is a measure of maturity. Even if what you say is, "I should have it done on Thursday," that's as good as giving your word. Don't over-sell yourself just to appease someone, especially when there is a decent chance that it won't happen.

One of the unique times when a commitment can be altered is when new information comes to you from the person that you said yes to. For example, if I was asked for a ride to the airport on Saturday morning at 10 am, to which I had said yes, I am committed to that appointment. If new information arises and that person comes to me and tells me that the plane will not be there until 2 pm, I am no longer obliged to my initial yes. Although I said yes to taking them to the airport, I was not offering to take them any time of day and clear my entire schedule. Perhaps I am still available to drive them, in which case, I don't see the harm in recommitting to the newly appointed time.

Clarifying this seems to be needed because it can be misunderstood what "keeping a yes" actually entails. When you give your word, it needs to mean something. It needs to have the support of your character and history of keeping your "yes." There should be a purposing to keep your "yes" commitment with all that you have. It is not a matter of mere convenience and hoping to find a justification that will suffice for you not keeping it because you didn't want to. The same application goes for business integrity.

WHAT IS A YES?

As I grew up, I observed my grandpa make business deals with a handshake. I even saw him buy real estate with this method. To him a handshake was his word, and it was as good as writing it in stone. He always told me how important keeping my word was.

Sadly, a handshake isn't what it used to be, and a yes isn't what it used to be either. A perceived *yes*, like, "I don't see why not"—is not a yes. "That should work," isn't a *yes* either. To be safe, never attach an expectation to anyone's future performance.

Listen precisely to what the other person is saying. "Coulds," "Woulds," and "Shoulds" mean absolutely nothing anymore. Most people take it for granted that these are promises. Or even, "I'll make it right next time"... Always ask, what do you mean? Even if it makes you look stupid.

That said, you need to understand—myself included—that saying you're going to do something is the same as saying, "I promise." Again, just because you literally didn't say "I promise" doesn't mean that your word isn't on the line. Trust me; you don't want to lose your word. When people don't trust you, you have lost everything.

Telling the Truth

It's very easy to lie to get ahead. Lying can help you sell products, and get a raise, but don't cross that line.

As you are already familiar, snowball effects are hard to stop once they get rolling. Lying is another one of those snowball-building occurrences. Each lie not only compounds upon the one before it, but it builds momentum quickly. The main difference with lying is that it really only takes one lie to get the ball rolling. Don't be a liar. Why? The obvious answer remains: the more that you lie, the less trusted you are. The less trusted you are, the more you will lose.

Covering up lies makes everything messier. Quite honestly, there is not a blanket of falsehoods big enough to cover up the mess you have made before a few lies are revealed. The truth will be found, and you will be blacklisted. Ask yourself, is my character worth it?

Part 5:

DREAM BIG

20. DREAM VERY BIG!

Now that we have gone over how to make more time, gain more wisdom, build wealth, and acquire knowledge, it is time to use our imaginations. It is time to learn how to dream big.

If you can't imagine it, how can you work toward it?

Think of your biggest dream, and then take it two to three steps further. How great will it be to get a raise? Well, that's a start, but how about this question? What if you could make a million dollars in the next five years? That's better. How about, wouldn't it be cool to make a million dollars in one minute? Do you think that it's possible? I've known of people who have.

How big is your imagination? For most, it is not very good. After you read the last paragraph, what were you thinking in your head? You were probably thinking, *ha! Yeah right! A million dollars in one minute?* If that's you, your imagination is not big enough. If you can't conceive it in your mind, it's not going to happen. This part of the book will help you dream big.

Begin to ask yourself questions like, *Wouldn't it be cool if?* Or, *What if...?* I ask myself these kinds of questions throughout the day, every day! I think these questions, and I ask other people around me these questions.

These are the same questions that I asked myself growing up. Wouldn't it be cool to tour with a band around the nation? Wouldn't it be cool to live on a cruise ship and travel the world? What if I could use the internet to create passive income? These are pretty lofty dreams. Or at least, they were until I accomplished them! Now, I think even bigger! Once you start accomplishing goals, your "big dreams" don't seem so big anymore.

AMBITION

I am an extremely ambitious person. As a child I played every sport I could possibly play, became an Eagle Scout, and did anything and everything I could possibly do. Sam Walton was way more ambitious than me, though. He was an Eagle Scout at age thirteen. In contrast, I had earned it four days before my eighteenth birthday, which was the deadline.

Be the very definition of ambitious.

Follow the principles and suggestions in this book, and Bob's your uncle. (You'll have to look that phrase up later.)

BE SPECIFIC

There is an expression in the hunting world, "aim small, miss small." If you aim at an animal, you might miss it. But if you aim at a specific part of the animal, you'll still hit the animal. Therefore, make your ambitions very specific and you will have a better chance of reaching the overall goal.

Set short, medium, and long-term goals. What are you goals for the next hour? Day? Week? Month? Year? Five years? Set short, medium, and long-term goals.

Goal setting builds hope for the future. What do you have to lose by setting goals that can be changed?

You have more to lose if you don't make goals.

AMBITION IS RELATIVE

Is ambition good or bad? It depends on what time era you are living in; words change meaning over time. Ambition is neither good nor evil. It is subjective. 'Ambitious' comes from the Greek word for 'both,' and referred to people trying to live for themselves and the kingdom of God.

Today the standard for what is ambitious is different depending on who you ask. For a small town citizen, flying to Paris could be ambitious. Some people live in Paris, so being in Paris isn't too ambitious at all for them. Some dream of going on a cross-country trip to some far away state. Some drive across the country for a living.

What is ambition? Like I've said, ambitious originally meant, 'both.' Later it was used in Greek literature to describe someone who practiced... or who ran for a political office. Now it refers to someone who aspires to be more and to do more.

Ambition is relative to each individual. Flying to California and putting your feet in the Pacific Ocean might be an ambition for some, but not for others.

You Have To Want It

Why do we do the things we do? We all do what we believe is in our best interest at that moment. Perhaps children don't want to go to school, but they actually do want to; either to avoid bad consequences or to achieve your long term goals of being literate.

We all do what we want to do. Let me state it this way; we must do what we want to do. You cannot do what you don't want to do. We are all slaves to our desires; even when people break the law.

Simply put, you have to want it. You must believe that it is in your best interest. There has to be a level of desperation. How bad do you have to want it? You have to want it bad enough to do something about it. If you want something bad enough you will make intentional actions toward that goal.

Life is very much like climbing a mountain. Some get to a certain point and become complacent, but only 1% climb to the very top.

Most stop at a certain point because they know the effort and trouble that they will have to go through to get any higher. The weather is always more intense at the top of the mountain. There's more responsibility and there's a lot more wind.

Bottom-Mountain Thinkers
Even with the effort, you might not make it to the top; so why try? Work doesn't always equate to success.

Middle-Mountain Stoppers
Most people settle mid-mountain. They're not willing to go to the top and endure the sacrifices or challenges. Maybe they're not prepared emotionally; maybe they're not strong enough to climb higher. We know that you do need money to meet your needs in this world, and maybe you have enough to make your ends meet, so why go any higher? This is the thought of many individuals.

For most people the effort it takes to reach the top isn't worth it, but they still want to be rich; hence the existence of gambling and the lottery.

So...you're on a mountain; you can see the top and you can see the bottom. Do you keep going, stay where you are, or turn back?

How bad do you want it? Is it worth it to you? I say it is. You just need to know how to get to the top.

Paying the Price

I knew that I wanted to move to Los Angeles. I had planned on driving my car, so I took it to our family mechanic to see if it would make it across the country. I ended up putting most of my savings into fixing the car. While the car was being fixed I was planning out my route with my mother in the lobby (they just so happened to have a big map on their wall). I had friends in different states along the way from previous travels with whom I was going to stay.

It wasn't even a week later before the car had another issue; a more expensive problem. It turned out that I wasn't driving to California after all, so I asked my mother when I was going to lose my free flights (I had free flights, but her company was acquired by another corporation, and they recently changed the rules). She told me that they would be gone by the end of the year.

Now knowing that I was traveling without a car, I needed to find out the exact date that I would lose my free flights. Instead of two months, I only had a couple of days. I soon discovered that it was in my best interest to fly out first thing in the morning.

I packed all night (I slept for about forty minutes). Then, when I finally arrived in Los Angeles, I was very sick from a lack of sleep (my body doesn't do well when it's tired).

Leaving the airport, I now was going to attempt to rent a room in a stranger's house. That only worked out for about three days. Then, after staying with my new buddies for two weeks, I was sleeping on the floor inside of a borrowed sleeping bag; sharing a tiny room with someone who was very different from me (it's a long story). To summarize, it took me about a year to get on my feet, and I had to work a lot of manual labor jobs.

I also had a culture shock like you wouldn't believe. So many emotions were flowing through my veins.

Why did I go through all that trouble? I had my heart set on attending the world's best seminary to sit at the feet of the finest theologians. I had been accepted to The Master's Seminary, which was under the leadership of John MacArthur. Attending Grace Community Church for me was like Disney World is to a child.

Though I went through all of that trouble, I would do it again in a heartbeat.

Is it worth it? It usually is.

Seriously Determined

You have to force your dreams into reality—I stole that phrase from the back of one of my T-shirts.

Do you remember the story I shared with you about my troublesome move to California? I found out that I couldn't drive, so I used my last free flight. Well...if it wasn't for my determination, I would have never had the diligence to pursue going on the terms that I did. I mentioned some of the sacrifices, but neglected to tell of the duration. (If it wasn't for my determination, I wouldn't have endured for so long.) I knew what I wanted, and there wasn't anything that would deter me from my goal.

Nothing x Nobody = Everything

This phrase (nothing x nobody=everything) refers to the premise of evolution, but most believe that it applies to becoming wealthy. They believe that they will write a song, join the NBA, or win the lottery, and become wildly rich. But as I will repeat in this book, the real equation to prosperity is:

Money + Time + Knowledge + Wisdom = Living Your Dreams

21. DARE TO DREAM

Every partnership usually has a dreamer and a realist. You need both for a good balance. You need the dreamer so that there are lofty goals to chase after. The dreamer is not easily discouraged. If you find yourself saying, "Wouldn't it be cool, if..." then you're the dreamer.

Maybe you define a dreamer as someone who fantasizes. I'm going to redefine it for you. A dreamer doesn't necessarily have his or her head in the clouds. A dreamer simply sees possibilities and seeks to attain them.

You also need the realist, also known as the skeptic. If you find yourself saying, "Yea, but..." it's probably you. The skeptic will keep the dreamer grounded in reality, and they will help flush out a step-by-step plan of how to accomplish the high and lofty goals. Maybe this person will use smaller goals to get closer to the end goal. They are the game planners.

The downfalls of skeptics are many. They can't attain greatness because they don't aim for it. Also, they might discourage the dreamer. The dreamer has to be stronger than the realist in order to reach his or her fullest potential.

If you don't have the dreamer, then you don't have any chance of success because the skeptic really won't try anything, that's why they are called skeptics. They don't think anything will work. One of you has to believe that the big goal is possible. The dreamer infuses hope.

Downfalls of dreamers can include thinking so unrealistically that you never reach your goals, and you're stuck in this limbo state of false hope. Like moving to Hollywood to pursue acting, but you take a server job at a restaurant. You never become a famous actor, but you never give up hope, so now you live your

Dream Big Live Bigger

entire life as a server. Don't be a dreamer that acts off of mere emotion and haste in decisions.

Dreamers and Skeptics can both be analytical. A lot of people make fun of analytical people by saying, "You think too much. You just need to relax." Simply don't pay attention to them because being analytical allows you to process complex information and apply it. You must be able to analyze data, such as written information, oral information, or sub-textual information. You must be analytical, and both dreamers and skeptics can be.

Being analytical allows you to be creative. The artist must analyze a skyline with all of its majestic colors before making a masterpiece. The artist must understand balance, proportions, shades, and color theory which is what an analytical mind can do. Don't put yourself or others into a box; you can be analytical, creative, and also a dreamer. What matters is that you take initiative no matter how you are designed.

Some Dreams are Only Dreams

Without discouraging you, the probability is that you will not accomplish all of your goals in life. If you do, you're not thinking big enough. Not all dreams will come to fruition, but imaginations are required to make any dreams come true.

Some dreams need to be given up. Say you want to be in a rock band and tour the world, but it's been twelve years and you are homeless...maybe you need to set that goal aside for now and work on a new dream with resources that are more related to your capabilities. Start with short-term goals.

Potential

What is the etymology of the word 'potential'? 'Potent' is Latin for 'being able to.' Over time, 'potent' became 'potentia,' meaning 'power.' We use the word 'potent' all the time today to mean 'power.' We say God is 'omnipotent,' meaning all powerful.

We need to live out our power—our potential. Why wouldn't we? If you knew that you could walk, you wouldn't crawl or scoot; of course, you would walk! Why don't we use our abilities to their fullest?

No one knows their full potential. No one knows what they're fully capable of. We learn about ourselves one accomplishment at a time. You have no idea what you're capable of accomplishing. Therefore, begin now to set higher goals for yourself. Think bigger than you ever have. Discover for yourself what your potential is one accomplishment at a time.

Aspirations

What did you want to be for Halloween? If you are a male, you wanted to be a superhero. If you are a female, you probably wanted to be a princess or something to that nature.

Children dream bigger and aspire to loftier things than adults do. Why is that? Is it simply because adults have a more realistic view of life? No, I say that we are taught either directly or indirectly to settle for the status quo. Maybe children are taught that they can be anything they want to be by their parents, but once they go to school it is a different story. Perhaps their teachers tell them to settle or maybe the bullies at school tell them. Hopefully, this book will bring you back to your more ambitious days. I can't promise that you will become superwoman or the next batman—they don't exist, but with enough time, money, wisdom, knowledge, and God's providence, you can become a princess or something equally great.

What does the word aspire mean? Well, the word "inspire" means that something external is giving you breath. The word *expire* means to breathe your last breath, so *aspire* means to pronounce with audible breath. To aspire means to declare a goal. You can aspire to anything. Have high aspirations.

Break the Mold

Hysteresis (pronounced hiss-ter-EE-sis). "Technically, the term describes the tendency of materials to snap back to their original shape once the pressure being applied is removed."[23] All of us need to change because no one is perfect. In order to change, we need to break the mold, and not snap back into our old habits. This is one of the hardest things you'll ever do.

When I speak in front of a crowd or give one-on-one advice to an eager listener, I notice that they begin to follow my advice right away. Then, as time goes on, they snap back into their old habits. We need to get beyond the status quo. If you want to change your socioeconomic class, you can. It is possible. Unless you are being held captive or are in some other extreme situation, you can break the mold.

What is the first step to breaking the mold? It is difficult to break because it is not pliable like our dreams tend to be—unless you are dead set on them. The mold is usually hardened; it takes a radical step to break it.

You will find the principles in this book difficult to apply perfectly because it is difficult to change habits. So, as you read this book, remember that you are not merely trying to acquire information. You are attempting to form new habits and a new way of life. That will require time and persistence and daily application. So refer to this book often.[24]

Blazing Your Own Trail

The most difficult aspect of breaking any mold is when you are the first to do something. Blazing your own trail is scary to say the least, and it takes a lot more creativity.

I was the first Eagle Scout in my entire family tree; the first to get a Bachelor's degree; the first to travel the world on my own; the first to do a lot of things. My point is that I had to learn how to blaze my own trail.

Imagine yourself hiking with your family, but once you and your family get to a certain point, your family just stops. Most people would stop where their families stop because to go farther means that your family isn't there to help anymore. There could be dangers, and you might not be prepared to go farther. You would be autonomous; all on your own.

It's not that your family doesn't want to help, they just don't know how because they haven't gone where you are about to go. It's scary. There is risk involved.

I have repeatedly blazed trails and gone places where my family wished they could help more, but simply couldn't. They couldn't give me advice and tell me what to avoid and how to prepare.

When you blaze trails and do things no one in your entire family has ever done, you have to want it. It takes determination, but every step you take and every goal you reach doesn't seem as scary as the one before. You will become more mature; it forces you to grow up.

Where the Green Grass Grows

Most people know John Newton as the writer of the song, "Amazing Grace." Less know that he was a captain of a British slave ship for many years. Even less know that he actually became a slave for fifteen months.

According to the book *Slave* by John MacArthur—highly recommended—Newton met a fellow passenger who happened to be a wealthy merchant in Africa. Supposing that he could become rich working for him, Newton left the ship and stayed in Africa. Through a series of events, Newton lost favor with his boss and things took a turn for the worse. According to Newton, "I was, in effect though without name, a captive, and a slave myself...I was rather pitied than scorned by the [lowest] of slaves." Newton thought that the grass was greener in Africa, but in the pursuit of wealth, he, himself became a captive of another.[25]

Is the grass *always* greener on the other side? No, not *always*, but sometimes it is. I recommend gathering as much information as possible before visiting the other side. If the grass is greener, then I would most definitely recommend going there. In Newton's case, the grass wasn't greener, and he made an ill-informed decision based on his desire to get rich quick.

Don't risk everything to move to a new country, or make a significant change without knowing if the grass is greener.

NOW OR NEVER

Don't put off a trip if you can take it now. You probably won't be able to take it in the future.

This principle applies outside of just your opportunities. It can be applied by you in business as well. The shorter the period of time between the offer and the purchase there is the better. An example is if you are pitching to investors, or if you are hiring someone. Ask them if they accept. If they say, I need more time, say, "I understand, well just give me an answer by tomorrow at 10 am."

The timing of things really matters. Do your best to hold yourself to this principle. Respond quickly to emails. Don't miss opportunities because you hesitated too long or because you simply failed to act. Make it a habit to take action.

22. DON'T STOP YOURSELF

Many middle-aged people realize that they didn't live to their full potential. They begin to doubt that they will ever reach their goals, so they are forced to reflect and to readjust. This is called middlescence.[26] This is what we want to avoid at all costs.

When pursuing a goal, especially an ambitious one, don't stop yourself. If you don't reach a goal, let it be because something else stopped you. Always see your goals to their end. If you could interview the future you, a twenty year older version of you, wouldn't you be encouraged if you had lived an ambitious life? If the opposite was true and you stopped yourself from accomplishing your goals, wouldn't you be disappointed in yourself because you knew that all of that potential was wasted?

Let's think about the life you have lived so far. If you wrote a book about your life, would anyone want to read it? The point is, to do everything in your power to achieve your goals, and let something else stop you. Let it be something external, not internal.

Let the Market Decide

If you have an idea for a product or service, don't allow yourself to be the judge of its success. Put it out into the marketplace and let the market decide if it's good or bad. You might think that you have a really stupid idea, but it might sell like crazy.

Reading the market can be confusing at times. It can be a difficult decision on whether or not you should try to launch a product that already exists. In a sense, there shouldn't be any new products in the marketplace. This is because there are giant corporations who are working day and night making their existing products better. They have millions of dollars devoted to product research and development. In order for your new product to be introduced, it must be so much better than the competition that it punches its way into the market. Your product must make the customers' everyday more convenience, help them improve their health, make them happy, or deliver some other value.

Sometimes the market may show oversaturation, but you may be surprised at how a product tailored just right and advertised at the perfect time can become the hot new thing. Don't shoot your ideas down. Let the market decide.

Pipe Dreams

The phrase "Pipe Dreams" originated in the nineteenth century in reference to dreams experienced when people smoked from an opium pipe. I would not encourage people to have pipe dreams.

I have always had pretty lofty goals. I was part of a leadership academy and during one session we had to write down our goals for the next five years. One of my goals was to be a millionaire. Everyone laughed at me. Maybe they couldn't conceive the thought of me being a millionaire, or maybe the timeframe didn't seem realistic.

Don't let anyone tell you that you're aiming too high. You have to believe, and be utterly convinced that you have the capabilities to do it. You can't just *think* it's possible; you can't just *think* you are able to do it. You have to be convinced that you can, it's the only way.

Don't let others discourage you for any reason, *ever*. Bullies put people down. *Only* bullies put others down. Anyone can be a bully: parents, siblings, friends, classmates, politicians, teachers, coaches; you name it. Most of the time when bullies pick on you (in the context of setting goals) they don't have big dreams, and probably won't make it past their socioeconomic status anyway. You might hear, "Yeah right! You can't do that!" Or, "Good luck with that one." (*Said sarcastically*)

You can't live your life for the approval of others, and you definitely can't let people tell you that you can't do something! The problem is that you can't stop people from putting you down. The solution is to use those put-downs as gasoline to fuel your ambitions. My response was always *"Just watch me"*.

Many people want to tell you that it's not possible because it makes them feel justified for not trying. If they can convince one more person that it's not possible to do X, Y, and Z, then their skepticism is reinforced. They think, "see, it's not possible," and they feel better about themselves. It's kind of sick. Plus, they want to convince you that it's not possible so that you don't show them up and make them look bad.

REASONS PEOPLE DON'T HAVE HIGH GOALS INCLUDE:

Complacency...

All too often people become content with living a passive life. Not seeking any goals and not living actively is better known as complacency. There is always room to grow, so despite a feeling of contentment, this is the rare case that you don't want to be self-proclaimed as 'content.' Why? Because you aren't actually content. Contentment is an acceptance of your circumstances and where you are at, but it doesn't make itself known by means of passivity.

You can be fully content, yet aggressively pursuing bettering yourself and your situation. Complacency is a prideful satisfaction with where you are or who you are. Complacent people don't seek growth. Complacent people don't have dreams that they work toward.

Being a homebody...

Everyone is different in the ways that they find comfort. Some people find comfort in traveling while others love the warmth and safety found in their home; sometimes becoming emotionally unable to leave home.

Whichever type of person you are, you can still set high goals and seek to obtain them. I know of a handful of individuals and even families that are crippled by their desire to be at home and do nothing outside of it. Well, there are still goals that can be obtained while staying at your house. You don't need to give up any comforts to reach some goals. You just need the internet and a bank account.

Don't Live For the Approval of Others

People will waste money buying athletic shoes at full price because those particular shoes are "cool." Unless you are being paid to promote a brand of shoe, don't worry about it. The private label brand will work the same. Starting now, don't care about keeping up with the latest fashions.

Living free from society's pressures to stay trendy will liberate you in general. Seeking approval from others is enslaving, and will stop you from reaching your full potential.

"There is nothing else that so kills the ambitions of a person as criticisms from superiors." –Charles Swabb

If you are sensitive to criticisms from others, simply don't tell anyone what your goals and dreams are on until they have been met successfully. Only tell people who you need to accomplish the goal. The fewer failures people know that you have the better. They eventually won't take you seriously. When people know of repeated failure it ruins your credibility.

Constantly seeking approval is stressful. When you fall short, which you will, it can be debilitating. Even if you don't make a mistake, others will still have their impression of you and hold you to their standard. Not meeting other people's unreasonable standards is a sure way to discouragement. Start living for the best that you can offer and help yourself by not adding unnecessary stressors to life. Find encouragement in your small wins and your potential for growth.

People have a bias, and it is possible that there is nothing you could ever do to meet their standard anyway. Some just might not like you. That's quite alright. You will never have to be reliant on one individual's approval when you have created raving fans elsewhere.

Victim's Mentality (No Excuses)

Never let your past hold you back.

Most people use their past or their current circumstances as an excuse of why they don't apply themselves or why they don't dream big. Well, I was born deaf, legally blind, I have scoliosis, one leg is longer than the other, and the list of my deformities goes on from there. So what? I had a couple of surgeries, had speech therapy for three years, and I got LASIK surgery. I still walk really funny, but that didn't stop me from being really good at sports; it didn't stop me from anything actually.

You might have to overcome a few obstacles, but that just means you have to try harder, that's all. I know of a quadriplegic who became a nationally recognized speaker and started a very successful non-profit organization. I also know of a person who has no arms and no legs, but still swims and has his full independence.

There is an attitude that believes that we are the victims of our circumstances. Of course, there are quotes that combat this, and they are numerous, but still people cling to the notion that they are a victim. We like to take on this mentality that we have no way of escape and that we are the way we are because of the circumstances we have been put through.

I will tell you now that there is no just excuse for behaving improperly and unwisely; or on the positive side, there is *no* excuse for not being successful.

I suppose this could tie in well with the fact that you are a victim of your own success. You choose to be successful, or you choose to sit back and play the victim in life. Whichever you decide will determine your outcome. Don't be convinced that there is no way to take the reins and steer yourself out of your circumstances. Until you have sailed, keep trying. Like I've said before, giving up is *not* an option and *nor* is having a victim's mentality.

Sink or Swim

Life is sink or swim.

Unless you have a floatation device, it's one or the other my friends. Don't be caught with excess weight causing you to sink. Don't get caught not knowing how to swim. You are the reason you sink, and you are the reason you swim.

Also, others that are sinking by choice will try to hold onto you, so swim well enough to either pull them up with you or relinquish their grasp on your life.

Don't Stop Yourself

There are certain seasons in life that you may find yourself being pulled undercurrent. Times when you are beginning to sink, you need to swim harder and keep enduring until you're afloat. Follow all the principles I'm teaching you, and even if life does drag you down, you won't be down for long. You *will* bounce back.

23. MATURITY

This is the last, but certainly the most important Life Lesson. It is also the most difficult to apply: maturity.

Mature persons are few and far between. Maturity is gold. No, it is priceless. Strive for maturity.

I wish I could say that making more money makes someone more mature. I wish I could say the more you make, the harder it is to offend you, a.k.a. get your feelings hurt. I wish I could say that making more money helps you make better decisions, but it doesn't. Giving more money to a teenager only enables that teenager to do more immature things, but that teenager will not make better decisions. One will only be as wise with his money as he is mature. The more money one has, the more the character is shown of that person.

Protecting Our Pride

If we don't get treated the way we expect to be treated, then we will throw a fit. We will become personally offended. Why? We believe consciously or subconsciously that throwing a fit will make the other person recognize how you should be treated. Conclusion, becoming personally offended and throwing a fit and getting mad and angry is to protect our pride. We literally *need* others to treat us the way we want to be treated, and if they don't, we will do everything in our power to make them do so.

This principle is not age specific. Adults throw fits and get their feelings hurt just as many times as a five-year-old does.

Mature people don't throw fits. They also know how to take ownership of their actions—and the consequences of them. Never use other people as scapegoats. Admit when something is, or at least partially is, your fault. When it is partially your fault, try to take full responsibility. This is the mark of truly mature person.

You cannot personally offend a humble person!

Mature people don't get their feelings hurt or get personally offended. 'Maturity' doesn't easily lose its cool or become offended. It stays cool, calm and collected, and it makes sound decisions. Negative emotions cloud decision making. Successful people need a calm, steady mind to collect as much information as they can before making decisions.

Mature people don't personalize things. They do not make decisions on a personal basis or because their feelings were hurt. There are almost no emotions involved when making big decisions. When life throws us big decisions, we need to be ready to choose which road to take. We need to be mature.

No Whining

Complaining shows a lack of maturity, and just because you begin your complaining with the phrase, "I am not complaining, but..." or "I don't mean to complain, but..." doesn't fix the fact that you actually are. Mature people maintain their composure, and they find the silver lining.

Spend as little of time as possible complaining, and even less time listening to others complain.

Venting is the complainer's best friend. When you vent, you air out all of your complaints to those listening. Both find their roots in a grumbling and discontented heart. *Both are a burden to those around you.* Believe it or not, your venting not only wears on others, but it shapes their perspective of you. Trust me; you don't want to be forever labeled as "the complainer." And it doesn't take that many complaints in venting sessions to earn that title, either.

This label is a repellant to success and a sure way to lose respect from others. Why is this? No one wants to be around the person that finds the bad in every situation. And most people don't care about your negativity. You will attract people when you complain, but it won't be successful people. Other complainers will flock to you and add to your whining. In fact, you will get stuck with them, and now your label is that much bolder because of the individuals you accompany yourself with.

If you have ever heard someone tell you that venting is healthy, then you definitely want to read what I'm about to tell you. Venting is not healthy. Okay we're done with that topic, right? Well, if you must know more, venting doesn't release your anger or "frustration" (frustration is socially acceptable term for anger).

What venting does do, however, is embitter your heart further. Unless you think on truth, you will compound that anger. This deeper anger then becomes too rooted to get rid of. You think that you released anger through your vent session, but in reality, you stored it as bitterness (which is a more complex form of hate).

Don't take time away from someone else's day to get all of your negativity off of your chest. Instead, take some quiet time to yourself to meditate and refocus on truth. It won't be a waste of time. Handle your emotions. The more that you practice dwelling on what is true of every situation, and not assuming the worst of others, the less time you will need to meditate.

Therefore, refraining from complaining in every sense will ultimately save you time and stress.

Self-Centeredness is *Not* Mature

Do you like talking about yourself, maybe too much? Do you ever start a sentence with, "I don't want to brag, but..."

Do you always start your sentences with 'I,' or do you focus your thoughts and actions toward yourself? Are you easily offended? I'm sure you are going to say 'No,' but what if I asked your coworkers?

In life, there are two kinds of people: those who are humble and those who are about to be humbled.

Never exalt yourself.
Avoid being narcissistic by only telling people about your accomplishments *unless* you have a pertinent point.

And...

Whenever you do talk about your accomplishments, never use the word "I did it" or, "I did this." Always use the word "we." Always recognize those people who have helped you. The chances of you doing it alone will be slim.

Do you always have to be right?
Are you answering this question with a, 'NO!" because you can remember a time when you asked for forgiveness? Or are you answering, 'NO!' reactively because you are defending yourself? Everyone has a desperate need to be right. It takes self-control and humility to back down from an unnecessary argument.

The biggest and most obvious manifestation of this kind of pride is when someone has to have the last word. Growing up, I always had to have the last word; hopefully, I've tapered that down a bit, but it is a tendency in *all* of us.

Having the ability to back down and let the other person have the last word is absolutely essential. This skill will help you grow your network, get promotions, and start partnerships. These alliances will then open doors that simply didn't exist. The irony is that when you stop focusing on yourself and always being right, you bless yourself.

Constructive Criticism

It is very hard to embrace and welcome criticism because it hurts our pride. In our pride, no one likes to be told what to do and when to do it. Humans naturally tend to dislike correction. I've met people who *claim* that they like correction, but few actually do. It takes humility to listen and implement corrections. Openly taking correction greatly diffuses a situation that would normally turn into a fight.

Don't ask for constructive criticism if you aren't truly ready to receive it. One of the quickest ways to embitter yourself against someone is to ask for a correction too soon. It seems ironic that we would ask for help, but be angry when we get it. Yet, with hearing a critique on ourselves, that is the very thing that happens. Know yourself. Know how weak you are and know when you have brought yourself to the point where you are ready to hear, "the bad news."

How will you know when you are ready?

I can't guarantee that you will know when you are ready. Sometimes it is trial and error. Sometimes you think you are prepared for the worst of corrections, but when it comes, you instantly find yourself ready to fight or justify your way out. I will say, don't coddle your pride. Take correction and honestly try to develop from it.

Yes, perhaps they have their facts misaligned. Perhaps they are missing a key piece of information as to why you performed in the manner that you did. Maybe if they were in your shoes, they too would see that your decision was the most strategic given your resources; maybe not. No matter what –right or wrong – you need to be able to hear other perspectives and not become offended.

This is and always will be easier said than done. I recall one of the best pieces of advice given by a previous mentor. He said to a large group of couples, "taking correction is like trying to swallow a pill the size of your fist." Imagine that! Reproof, a.k.a. correction, is a hard pill to swallow, though what it offers is beneficial to the body. You know you need to take the pill that was administered to you, but you have to gear up and psych yourself for what is about to occur.

Understanding and fully accepting criticism does take time and need I say... practice. Every reproof should have a sharpening effect if you are humble. If you don't understand and accept criticism, it can make you dull or callus. Becoming callus is a huge hindrance to your growth. Decide ahead of time that you want to grow, admit that you need to grow, and it will make the pill that much smaller.

To put it into another illustration, fire refines gold. When you want to purify gold, you heat it ten times over. Think of correction as a trial of fire that will refine your heart and life. Despite how the correction is given, be it in anger or in judgment, you can be purified by it. Allow the refining process to take its course in your life. Allow it to make you better.

Channel your energy:
Use constructive criticism as motivational fuel to accomplish something.

WHAT MAKES CORRECTION SUCH A HARD PILL TO SWALLOW?

We hate when other people view us differently than how we desire to be viewed. When this happens, our pride is struck, and we proclaim how great we are to ourselves, our coworkers, and even to the one who corrected us.

When someone corrects you, does it make you mad or annoyed? Are you raising your hand or mentally agreeing? You should be. I don't think any of us human beings are exempt from this defense of our pride.

Almost immediately following correction, we look for the nearest person in proximity to justify ourselves to. The justification is regarding why we were either unable to perform perfectly or why that person's opinion is faulty and unimportant. Even before we find that unsuspecting soul to vent to, we run a play by play in our own minds. We start with the facts, then wind up with one, two, or many reasons to support why we shouldn't have been corrected in that scenario. "If only they knew all of the information, they wouldn't be judging me." Well, I'm sure that's true, but it isn't the point. If only we spent more time applying the correction than we do justifying ourselves against it.

Feeding your pride will harm your success story.

DEFENDING OURSELVES BECAUSE OF OUR ASSUMPTIONS

Assumptions are the quickest and easiest way to feed our, "I'm right" prideful moment when we are corrected by someone.

Always keep in mind that you don't know other people's thoughts to know if they think lesser of you. It could easily be the opposite. They could care enough about you to ensure you know the best way of doing your task, etc. There is always someone who has gone before you that you can learn something helpful from. Be careful not to fall into the pit of being quick to judge your corrector's thoughts, motives, and conclusions. Welcome help from others without assuming the worst of their intentions or their conclusions of you.

Believing the best of others will help you receive correction without becoming embittered against the one giving it.

TACTFULLY GIVING CORRECTION

"Let no unwholesome word proceed from your mouth, but only such a word as is good for edification according to the need of the moment, so that it will give grace to those who hear."
–Ephesians 4:29

Never correct others in public...
Context is the underlying foundation of giving correction in a manner that is both skillful and loving. As we all have experienced, there are not many places that are suitable for giving correction. Never correct others in public. It's disrespectful, and normally people don't have the humility required to take correction properly. Therefore, you will offend

them. This results in a loss of an acquaintance, buddy, or even a sale.

Often you will have to wait for the proper time and place, but when you do, the outcome is vastly different than if you had been hasty. You want to set the tone for the reproof you are about to give. Practically speaking, you will want a place that offers little distraction, is quiet, and conducive to a potentially emotional discussion.

The point of correction is neither to provoke nor to belittle. It is for the sole purpose of helping the individual about to receive it and the situation for a positive outcome.

Don't give constructive criticism if the person already knows what they need to fix. It misses the point of being constructive. You're no longer building the individual up in something, but tearing them down. Correcting, in this case, will prove to be more discouraging than it is helpful.

Some bosses feel like they need to correct every one of their employees on everything they do. Yes, I am exaggerating, but there are many bosses who over-correct. These employees may feel that they already know what they did wrong and have implemented a means of correcting their mistake for the future. Coming in and telling this individual what they already know is like unknowingly beating a dead horse. Except in this, it has the power to provoke anger. Use discretion to determine if you need to advise or reprove others.

Don't correct in haste. If you want to share information that you feel is more accurate or will make them more efficient, then wait. Find a tactful way to convey your input. One way is to infuse it into a conversation that indirectly shares your insight with them.

Example:
Amber taught her friend, Sally how to better hydrate her hair. Sally listed the products she was using, but Amber felt that she would benefit more from using different products. Amber allowed time to pass and in the proper moment, she told Sally, "I just had my hair trimmed to get rid of my split ends. You can't avoid them, but when I use silk for pulling in the moisture and pair it with natural oil –like argan oil to lock it in –then it keeps my hair in a healthier state." No one was offended, and the constructive criticism was received.

A kind way of telling someone information is to preface it with, "I'm sure you already know this, but…" This alleviates any tension that could arise from others feeling like you are belittling them or assume they are uninformed.

Never correct someone when *you're* frustrated. Frustration is a euphemism for anger. (This is especially true when parents discipline their children. Never discipline children or correct someone out of wrathful anger.)

Be extremely hesitant to correct an older person, even in private. If you do, be very observant of their body language. If you sense any egos being offended, stop! They probably just can't handle constructive criticism. Everyone should be open to correction, regardless of their age, but read reactions.

Also, when giving constructive criticism, make sure that you are humble and aren't belittling them. It must be done in love.

Make sure you give them an encouragement sandwich.
By that I mean, give:

Encouragement
Correction
Encouragement

Maturity

Say something encouraging, then give them the edifying correction, then encourage them again. This is apparently an art and skill that needs to be practiced because either not many know about this tactic, or they are really bad at it.

Encouragement sandwich:
The sandwich must include only the normal ingredients. If it doesn't belong in the Peanut Butter and Jelly sandwich, don't include it. By this I mean, make sure that your encouragements are directly related to the correction.

If you are correcting someone on their pattern of wrathful anger toward their employees, don't give encouragement that has nothing to do with anger and kindness, such as their ability to play basketball. "Joe, you are really good at basketball, but sometimes in the office, you display really hateful speech when your employees make a mistake. I'm glad that you are improving your fishing skills as well." Joe will think you are ridiculous in your encouragement and might take more offense.

A better way of addressing someone with a pattern of anger would be to encourage them that they have improved in the frequency, but that their speech is still tearing down the employees and needs to be addressed. Followed by an encouragement that you are glad they typically realize their anger and apologize a few days following their outburst. That would be a more connected example of an encouragement sandwich.

What also helps is to let the person know that you have made the same or a similar mistake, or say, "I've done worse." Because it relays that there is grace for them to grow and that you are no better than them. This ensures that you are humble too. If you can't say, at least in your heart, that you have done worse, then you are not ready to correct that person.

Foolish People Get Mad

A lot of times people misunderstand, and rather than clarifying, they react on the misunderstanding in offense. This is part of making assumptions based off of your bias. Everyone is equipped with their personal bias that shapes the way that they interpret their environment. If the only times you have heard someone tell you, "I'm fine." is when they are angry and seeking for you to give them extra attention, then to hear a new friend tell you that they are fine, will trigger in your mind that they aren't.

You then might react the way you would if you thought they were angry at you when really they were communicating that they are simply that, fine. It's a rough example, but the point is that you will interpret people based on what you are familiar with until you become familiar with more variety. This is a fundamental reason why we can't view situations through a narrow perspective, and we must ask for clarification often.

Foolish people assume too quickly and react. Rather than becoming angry, it is always better to stay calm and begin to discern. If need be, you can clarify by asking, "What did you mean by that?" Even still, the other person may not be the best at communicating, and you can be on different understandings, so try to remain unbiased.

Keep in mind that when people don't understand what you are saying they might assume the worst. What was not intended to offend could be perceived as you making fun of them; simply because they didn't understand what you meant. If you offend someone who simply didn't understand what you meant, just clarify. If you are the person who got offended, ask the other person to clarify. Either way, we need to expect the best intent in others, regardless of our initial reactions.

Part 6:

THE RESULT

24. LIFE WILL CHANGE

The past is the past. Even though I've been on a lot of adventures, I wouldn't want to repeat the past, either to relive the good times or the bad. If I could get into a time machine and relive a period in my life, I wouldn't get in the machine at all. That is because life is so much better now than it ever has been. When you live your life to the fullest, every day will be the best day of your life. Tomorrow will always be better than yesterday.

I have never made fewer mistakes than now. I have never known more information, I have never been more mature, and I have never had more experiences. Today is way better than yesterday. Every day is an adventure. Every day something happens that changes my tomorrow.

Success is predicated on a series of choices. Begin to make a series of choices that lead you to success—and you already have by picking up this book.

When you begin to practice all of these lessons, life will change dramatically. Doors will fly open, and you will have so many stories. When you begin to make big moves in your life, you will live dreams you never knew you had.

You will be so knowledgeable and wise about different subjects that older people will ask you for advice.

You will not only change your life but those around you. I was heavily influential in getting a college to start an international business program. Due to my experiences and education, I was able to develop and construct the curriculum by merging two departments. Now students can get a degree in international business.

Charlie Baum changed the landscape of a small town by heading up the construction of the city library.

Dream Big Live Bigger

How many lives will you change? It *starts* by changing your life first.

Where will you be one year from now? How about five years? Thirty years? It's up to you. No one can live your life for you. What could you cut out of your life that is holding you down? If this book has helped change the way you think, change someone else's life by telling them about this book. Teach others the lessons from this book, especially children.

We teach best what we need to learn most. I needed the lessons in this book to take me from poverty to independence. They have shaped my life, and I hope that they will be used to shape the lives of others.

For the past six, people have been telling me to write a book. Well, here it is. Now it's time for you to write your own story.

A NOTE FROM THE AUTHOR

"The fear of the LORD is the beginning of
knowledge; Fools despise wisdom and
instruction" -Proverbs 1:7

Although these principles I have given are wise and will
generally help you to live bigger, it is my personal conviction
that true wisdom is ultimately only found in the fear of the Lord.
Romans 6 (cf. Galatians 1:1-10)

NOTES

[1]Carnegie, Dale. *How to Win Friends and Influence People*. New York: Simon and Schuster, 1981. Print.

[2]Bunyan, John, Robert Lawson, and Lucy Aikin. *Pilgrim's Progress*. Philadelphia, PA: J.B. Lippincott, 1939. Print.

[3]Fowler, H. W., F. G. Fowler, and James A. H. Murray. *The Concise Oxford Dictionary of Current English*. Oxford: Clarendon, 1964. Print.

[4]"Can You Train Yourself to Get by on Less Sleep?" *BBC*.N.p., n.d. Web. 30 Mar. 2016.

[5]Bits and Pieces, published by The Economics Press, Fairfield, N.J.

[6]Nichols, Ryan. "Thomas Reid." *Stanford University*. Stanford University, 28 Aug. 2000. Web. 30 Mar. 2016.

[7]Fleming, William. *Student's Manual of Moral Philosophy: With Quotations and References for the Use of Students*. London: Murray, 1871. Print

[8]"How Much Money Do The Top Income Earners Make?" *Financial Samurai*.N.p., n.d. Web. 30 Mar. 2016.

[9]Carnegie, Dale. *How to Win Friends and Influence People*. New York: Simon and Schuster, 1981. Print.

[10]Montaigne, Michel De. *Quotes and Images From The Works of Michel De Montaigne*. Place of Publication Not Identified: Project Gutenberg, 2015. Print.

[11]"The Definition of Worry." *Dictionary.com*. N.p., n.d. Web. 30 Mar. 2016.

[12]"The Definition of Habit." *Dictionary.com*. N.p., n.d. Web. 30 Mar. 2016.

[13]Carnegie, Dale. *How to Stop Worrying and Start Living*. New York: Simon and Schuster, 1948. Print.

[14]Everson, Carol A. "Sleep Deprivation and the Immune System."*Understanding Sleep: The Evaluation and Treatment of Sleep Disorders*. (n.d.): 401-24. Web.

[15]Hansen, Mark Victor., and Robert G. Allen. *The One Minute Millionaire: The Enlightened Way to Wealth*. New York: Harmony, 2002. Print.

[16]"Mothers Asked Nearly 300 Questions a Day, Study Finds." *The Telegraph*. Telegraph Media Group, n.d. Web. 30 Mar. 2016.

[17]"The Definition of Money." *Dictionary.com*. N.p., n.d. Web. 30 Mar. 2016.

[18]Blackwell, L. A., Trzesniewski, K. H., & Dweck, C. S. (2007). Theories of intelligence and achievement across the junior high school transition: A longitudinal study and an intervention. Child Development, 78, 246-263.

[19,20,21,22]Carnegie, Dale. *How to Win Friends and Influence People*. New York: Simon and Schuster, 1981. Print.

[23]Hansen, Mark Victor., and Robert G. Allen. *The One Minute Millionaire: The Enlightened Way to Wealth*. New York: Harmony, 2002. Print.

[24]Carnegie, Dale. *How to Win Friends and Influence People*. New York: Simon and Schuster, 1981. Print.

[25]MacArthur, John. *Slave: The Hidden Truth about Your Identity in Christ*. Nashville: Thomas Nelson, 2010. Print.

[26]Harvey, David T. *Rescuing Ambition*. Wheaton, IL: Crossway, 2010. Print.

Walton, Sam, and John Huey. *Sam Walton, Made in America: My Story*. New York: Doubleday, 1992. Print.

Giuliani, Rudolph W., and Ken Kurson. *Leadership*. New York: Hyperion, 2002. Print.